HORNELL HART

Your Share of God

Spiritual Power for Life Fulfillment

Englewood Cliffs, N.J.

PRENTICE-HALL, INC., 1958

PRINTED IN THE UNITED STATES OF AMERICA

98095

Contents

‡‡

iii

8 *Prayer Can Change Enmity Into Friendliness (Continued)*

9 *How to Conquer Temptation by Prayer* 112

10 *How to Win a Clean Conscience by Prayer* 131

Book *I*

The Great Adventure

Is Open to You

Chapter 1

Are There Unfilled

Needs in Your Life?

Would you like to find out why you are here?

Would you like to discover what the purpose of your life truly is, and what you are called upon to experience and to achieve?

Have you been lonely?

Are you hungry in spirit for something solid to believe in? Do you quite often get discouraged and feel defeated? Do you wonder sometimes whether life is really worthwhile and what it's all about?

Do you have need of power and wisdom higher than human?

Almost all of us believe that such a power exists. There are people, of course, who argue that the universe is merely blind, cold, indifferent, and mechanical. But all of us who think seriously about the problems of our own lives and the problems of the world realize that we need more light. If there *is* a power above all human power and a wisdom above all human wisdom, we need to learn how to tune in. Sometimes our need is desperate.

If any of these things are true of you, then we have a quest to carry out together. We have all met people who live life radiantly. They seem to have discovered the secret as to how to triumph over life's difficulties. They seem to have achieved solutions of the problems which everyone, sooner or later, has to meet. If life *can* be joyous, triumphant, and creative, then you and I want to know the secret. We want to know how to bring that kind of joy into our own daily living, and into the lives of those we love.

Do you need light?

We live in an age of science. Science makes people more and more sure about a great many material facts. We are more and more sure about how to build luxurious automobiles, how to raise more bushels of corn per acre, how to blow up cities on the other side of the world, how to cure and prevent some of the most deadly diseases, how to produce color television— and so on and so on.

But science has also been making many thoughtful people less and less sure about a lot of other things. In the Middle Ages, the Church could give a clear cut and unmistakable answer to all the great questions of life. Even as recently as the beginning of the present century, well-educated people felt confident that the teachings of the Church could give completely true answers about the great questions of life and death —about how to remake society, about how to abolish war, about divorce and crime, about sexual morality, about life beyond the grave, and about man's close relationship with Father God. Science, while it has made us far more sure about how to prevent polio and how to kill people wholesale, has made vast numbers of people less and less sure about many of the deepest and most vital problems of our lives.

If you feel that way, then we have an adventure to take together. You and I are fellow seekers in a great quest. If these mysteries of the universe can be unlocked, if these powers and spiritual values are to be had by humble and earnest seekers, then you and I want to join the search.

HERE ARE SOME QUESTIONS TO WHICH WE NEED ANSWERS

First let us set down a brief series of queries on which the basic meaning of life pivots:

1. *What is really worthwhile?* Are there any great imperishable goals that make life truly and richly worth living?

2. *What can we believe about God?* Is He an all-loving and all-powerful Father? Does He answer prayer? Does He in any sense guide destinies? Or is there merely an impersonal regulator that underlies the universe? Why is the world so full of suffering and evil?

3. *We die—then what?* Within a few years, your physical body and mine will be dead. What then will have happened to that which thinks "I" within you, and to that which thinks "I" within me? What will happen to our real selves when our brains die? Will these essential personalities of ours have been extinguished like a candle flame that has been blown out? Will we be wandering in some vague spiritual No Man's Land? Or will we be going onward in the great adventure, in an existence at least as vivid and real as that in which we now live?

It is not merely your personal survival and mine that matter. We want to know what has happened to that dearest one whose body died not long ago. What will happen to the personalities of those nearest and most beloved to you and to me when their bodies go down into the grave? Why cannot scientists give us any firm answer about whether there is a life beyond death?

4. How can we put religion to work?   Can we find a faith by means of which we can live triumphantly, no matter through what difficulties and disasters? How can prayer transform our lives? How can we find that heavenly life, here on earth, by means of which brotherly love and creative power can take possession of us?

5. Can Heaven come on earth?   Among first-century Christians, the most ardently longed-for goal appears to have been to go to Heaven. More recently, in the high tide of the social gospel, inspired leaders taught that heaven could be achieved on earth. How about it? What reality lies back of the heaven ideal, whether before or after death? Why cannot religion do something effective about war, about divorce, about juvenile crime, about dictatorship, about the cruelty, the greed and the hypocrisy that flourish so in the world today?

6. What about sin and failure?   How can people find freedom from feelings of guilt and inferiority?

Those are just a few of the questions to which you and I must have some sort of working answers if we are to go on living with vision and purpose.

TEST ALL THINGS; HOLD FAST TO THAT WHICH IS GOOD

Seven beliefs of power

We are not the first who have set out in this quest. Many have found answers which, for them, have lighted the torch of faith and have given the power for daily triumphant living. Here are seven beliefs which some have found to be both consistent with science and effective in opening up the spiritual life:

1. **God is real.**
2. **Prayer works wonders.**
3. **Death is a gateway to life more magnificent.**
4. **The leadership of the seers and prophets of all the ages is with us now, today.**

5. Science, when it speaks humbly and truly, is the voice of God.

6. The burden of proof is on those who deny these things.

7. God has magnificent work for you to do, and for me, and for every man, woman, and child who will listen.

If those seven things are true, then neither you nor I have any justification to feel discouraged or defeated or lonely. Life in its true reality is wonderful. You and I are here in the midst of a magnificent adventure.

Our shared quest

But are these seven things true? That is a question to which this book lights the way to an answer. Read it with an open mind and with alert and challenging intelligence. Try it out and see whether it works. That is what scientists do. They call it "testing hypotheses." Paul (he who is the hero of the Book of Acts, and who wrote the letters which form the core of the New Testament after the Book of Acts) said: "Test all things; hold fast to that which is good!" That is the method of every true scientist. Here, then, is an hypothesis for you to test:

Life for you and for me can have growing joy, growing achievement. All we have to do is to get more and more into tune with reality—find our places in the scheme of things, under God's guidance. All we need to do is to get into tune with the creative forces of this Universe, to understand, to be filled with the power, and to go forward. All things work together for good to those who thus love God.

So let us inquire, open-mindedly but searchingly, into the truth of the Seven Beliefs of Power.

DO ADVENTURE SPIRITUALLY!

There is a formula for successful living that is called "The Four Dont's and the Three Do's." If you can avoid the Four

Dont's and if you can live up to the Three Do's, you never need to get discouraged; you can always live courageously, with love and power.

Here are the Four Don'ts:

1. **Don't acquiesce ignobly.**
2. **Don't evade cravenly.**
3. **Don't attack vindictively.**
4. **Don't rush rashly.**

Each of the Four Don'ts warns against a way of misusing the God-given energy which surges up in your body and your mind when you are challenged by some difficulty or danger.

Here are the Three Do's:

1. **Do change menace to promise by courage.**
2. **Do find comrade and partner creators.**
3. **Do adventure spiritually.**

Often it seems terribly difficult to be courageous when the odds look overwhelming. Sometimes it seems as if it really were impossible to be friendly and cooperative when people around us are unreasonable, harsh, mean, unjust, and overbearing. We need aid above and beyond human help.

Do adventure spiritually!

A supreme secret is locked up in this third Do. To be courageous and cooperative without laying hold on spiritual guidance and power is to act like the young man who forms a friendship with a truly wonderful girl, but never goes forward into engagement and marriage. To adventure spiritually means to dare to act as though there is a Power above all human power and a Wisdom above all human wisdom—to act as if that Power and that Wisdom are yours for the asking and the seeking. To test that belief, and to hold fast to it if it proves to be good, is to adventure spiritually.

THIS, THEN, IS OUR CHARTED QUEST

Here in this first chapter we have been sketching a trail which we propose to follow through the perplexities and the problems of life in search for valid guidance.

You are called to this quest if you feel either or both of these two needs:

1. The need for help from a Power and a Wisdom higher than human;

2. Light on the great and basic problems of existence.

Questions to which we need answers include these six:

1. What is really worthwhile?

2. What can we believe about God?

3. We die—then what?

4. How can religion be put to work in your life and in mine?

5. Can heaven come on earth?

6. What about sin and failure?

Test all things is the working rule of applied courage, both in science and in religion. Hold fast to that which proves to be good. Seven beliefs of power have been emerging. Our shared quest is to test the hypothesis that these seven things are true.

Chapter 2

The Goal of Religion Is

Fulfillment of Life

TRUE RELIGION IS JOYOUS

The Song of the Angel, as related in the story of the first Christmas, includes these words: "Be not afraid; for behold, I bring you good tidings of great joy which shall be to all the people."

Jesus, in his last conversation with the Disciples before He was crucified, is reported to have said: "These things have I spoken unto you that my joy may be in you, and that your joy may be made full."

Paul said: "Let your hope be a joy to you."

Other religions also promise joy

Judaism (from whose scriptures Christians have taken the Old Testament) puts it thus: "Thou wilt show me the path of life. In Thy presence is fulness of joy." The Buddhist scriptures say: "Joy and gladness shall be yours, as you school yourself by day and by night in the things that are right." Con-

9

fucianism says: "Heaven sends down to thee long-enduring happiness, which the days are not sufficient to enjoy." The Hindu scriptures say: "May God breathe His balm on us, filling our hearts with joy!" Sikhism tells its followers: "He who hath found God in his heart is happy in mind and body."

Fulfillment of life is the clue

All the great religions hold out these promises of joy and happiness. How are such promises to be fulfilled? Jesus suggested the answer when he summed up the purpose of his life mission in these words:

"I have come that they may have life and have it to the full." To live life to the full is the essential road to true joy and satisfaction.

YOU CAN FIND FULFILLMENT OF LIFE BY ADOPTING GREAT PROJECTS

If you would find fulfillment of life—if you would learn to go forward on the road toward heaven on earth, and toward heaven beyond death, give yourself with all your heart and soul and mind and strength to two or three great projects.

But what is a project?

If you have chosen a life career, and if you find the career challenging, absorbing, and creative, then this is one of your basic, life-fulfilling projects.

If you have found your true love—if you have discovered how such a love grips your life, expands your heart, and challenges your achievements, then this courtship and this marriage have become a basic, life-fulfilling project.

If you have dreamed of having children, of the absorbing task of bringing new human beings into the world, and if you have begun to realize the perplexities, the difficulties, the possible agonies, and the rich fulfillment that can come from parenthood, then you have found another fundamental life-fulfilling project.

If you are stirred by dreams of beauty, and if you have persistently dedicated portions of your weeks and your years to bringing beauty into the world, then that is still another life-fulfilling project. The beauty may be the loveliness of flowers in a garden, or the thrill of human voices, or orchestral instruments blended into harmony, or the beauty of words brought together into poetry, drama, fiction, or some other form to stir the heart and mind. Or, the beauty may be that of pigments on a canvas or of shapes in clay or marble or architectural form. To create beauty is a life-fulfilling project.

Above and beyond your career, your marriage, your parenthood, your creative endeavors to bring beauty into the world—above and beyond all such undertakings lie the invitation and the challenge to the project magnificent. That project, which can enfold all others and which towers above and beyond them into eternity, is commitment to the spiritual adventure—going forward with open eyes and heart and mind into learning how to live the spiritual life, with fuller and fuller awareness of the Supreme and Eternal Consciousness in whom we live and move and have our being.

Let us now examine this guarantee that you and I can find fulfillment of life, that you and I can learn to live in heaven on earth and heaven beyond death if we will give ourselves wholeheartedly to two or three such projects, and if we carry them through to success. We have turned our minds briefly to five examples—a career, marriage, parenthood, artistic creation, and the all-encompassing spiritual adventure. Let us now look briefly at a fairly typical case.

SHE FOUND FULFILLMENT BY THE PROJECT METHOD

This woman has been married for more than 40 years. Let's call her Edith. Her father and mother were immigrants. He was a social idealist, a labor organizer, and a dedicated public servant. Her mother was deeply wrapped up in rearing her ten children. She wore herself out at it and died in middle life, at a time when the younger children were still in grade school.

Her brothers and sisters were her project before she married

Edith was keenly intelligent. She longed for an education. Indeed, her intensely burning ambition was to become a doctor. But the family income was too small for the huge needs of the growing children. Edith left school in the sixth grade and went to work in a factory. She, too, became a social idealist, pouring out her energies in channels quite similar to those in which her father had given such splendid service. And she devoted herself with a fierce enthusiasm to making life rich for her brothers and sisters.

This kept her utterly absorbed until she was 26 years old. She was an enthusiastic member of a social settlement that had been established in the working-class district near her home by a great state university. This settlement maintained a summer camp. One summer, while she was taking a weekend of country recreation at this camp, she happened to be sitting on the floor, playing with some children. In the midst of a game she felt that someone was staring at her.

Love at first sight gave her a new project

She looked up and saw a young man. She learned later that his name was Jeff. She had never seen him before, but suddenly she felt a deep, positive assurance. That night she told her best friend that she had that day met the man she was going to marry. It wasn't long before the young man himself reached the same conclusion. The very next day they went out canoeing together, found their way to a lonely island, and there, seated with their backs against the trees, they read poetry together. He, too, was 26 years old. He had an M.A. degree from the university. When his father heard that he was going to marry a factory girl who had left school in the sixth grade, he made a special trip to try to head off the wedding. The best response he could get was a promise from the couple that they would wait until the next year. This was September. They were married at nine o'clock in the morning on January first.

Edith was utterly happy. Jeff was earning less than she had been before she gave up her job to marry him, but she courageously started to work at furnishing their apartment, and at stretching his income to cover their modest needs. Within ten months she was also getting ready for their firstborn.

Four new projects were born to her

They had four children within five years. Jeff was an underpaid young professional man. After their fourth child was born, he accepted a position in a distant city. They used up all their money in moving. Jeff had only one presentable pair of trousers. They had no car, and he didn't even have an umbrella. It rained every day for the first two weeks. Every night Jeff would come home with his suit all draggled, and Edith would quickly heat the iron and press it out for the next day.

They could not afford a servant. Edith not only kept the house and cooked the meals. She did all the sewing, washing and ironing for her family, and in addition spent her evenings typing and retyping the manuscript of the heavy and voluminous textbook which he was writing.

Indeed, she kept urging him on in the hope that he might produce a book which would both establish his reputation and finance the family. He called her "my slave-driver," but at last his first textbook was published. The first royalty check was enough to make a down-payment on a car. They named the car "His Majesty," because it had come from royalty.

Her projects called for sacrifices

Of course, life wasn't usually smooth sailing. Problem after problem arose. Her husband's struggles, the children's schooling, the income which never seemed to catch up with the family needs—one thing piled up on top of another. But Edith was happy—deeply happy.

That the man she loved should succeed in his aspirations and in his profession became a supreme objective for her. At one time, when they, with two babies and another one on the way, were struggling along on a $3,000 salary, Jeff was offered a $2,000-a-year fellowship by means of which he might study for a Ph.D. degree. He assumed that the offer was impossible because of his family needs. When she heard about it she insisted on taking the $1,000 cut and putting her husband through the university, even though it meant living for 18 months, with the three children, in a two-room house, without a bath, which they rented for $15 a month.

She found guidance through the Inner Light

Both Edith and Jeff had been professed atheists when they married. One Saturday afternoon they were out walking, pushing a baby carriage that contained their three small children. (The fourth was already on the way.) They passed a meeting house with a sign which read: "Friends' Meeting, First Day Morning." He said: "These Quakers are so quaint! Let's go to meeting tomorrow and see what it's like!" So they and the children all went. And when the meeting settled into Silence, in the simple gathering place, they suddenly felt a Power, and began to know the reality of an Inner Light. Edith guided her life and her family, thereafter, by the aid of that Light.

Her children's families gave her new projects

All of her four children had high I.Q.'s. Each of them, of course, had to be sent through college. Edith was proud, and refused to ask for scholarships. Financial problems got deeper. They had to borrow up to the hilt on their insurance. Then, finally, one by one the children married. Now there were five families to look after instead of one. Edith gave all her heart to each of the ten grandchildren as they came into the world, and defended and nourished them just as she had her own. Her life seemed at times to have become a series of frantic long-distance phone calls from one son or daughter after another, telling how desperately Grandma was needed to tide the grown children and the grandchildren through some otherwise insoluble crisis. She loved every minute of it.

Her late-life project was creating a home of beauty

Between trips to the children's families she devoted herself —heart, mind and soul—to making beautiful the home in which she and her husband lived. They called it their "estate." It was a one-acre lot, carved by bulldozers out of a wooded hillside. Edith had herself designed the house, and she had acted as strawboss day after day while the house was being built. When she, Jeff, and a batch of grandchildren moved in through a sea of mud one winter day, triumph was high despite the fact —or because of the fact—that years of work lay ahead to make the place the utterly beautiful home of which she dreamed.

Thus was her life filled full

Why was Edith such a basically happy woman? Because she lost herself in a few lifelong objects, each of which was greater than herself. First it was shared with her father, her mother, her brothers and her sisters. The best attainable life had to be won for them, and her vital energy poured out with indefatigable enthusiasm toward that goal. Then it was the man she loved. Her husband's personal and professional success has been built on the foundations of her utter love, her forgiving patience, and her creative enthusiasm. Her children's lives have been carried through one threatened disaster after another until each of them has found his or her place in vital community service and in deep family joy.

Then the children, and later the grandchildren, became the objects of her supreme devotion. To help them find fulfillment of life was a project to which her energies were dedicated. Later, as the immediate urgency of the children's problems receded, the creation of a home that would shine with beauty and that should be a center of fellowship and of community service, became the project of her later years. Her life was filled to the full because she gave herself, with all her heart, to projects greater than herself.

TO FIND YOURSELF YOU HAVE TO
LOSE YOURSELF

Nineteen centuries ago the Great Teacher said: "He that saveth his life shall lose it, but he that loseth his life for my sake and the Kingdom's shall find it."

In modern times, Alfred, Lord Tennyson, in his *Idyls of the King*, told how the old magician Merlin had created an oaken chair that he called "Siege Perilous," "for there," he said, "no man could sit, but he should lose himself." When Sir Galahad saw the seat, and heard about its peril for good and ill, he exclaimed: "If I lose myself, I find myself!" and sat down.

This is an inherent principle of the universe

The fact that he who would find the life abundant must lose himself in something greater than himself is not an arbitrary rule thought up by preachers. Since long before the dawn of history, men have found fulfillment by uniting with women to form families. Families have found fulfillment by uniting with other families to form clans. Clans have formed tribes; tribes have united into nations; nations have formed empires and commonwealths. At the present stage in the world's history, we are watching and participating in a vast, groping endeavor to unite the nations, empires and commonwealths of the earth into a world-wide democracy.

You and I are living parts of that vast upbuilding process, in which units on every level find fulfillment by losing themselves in something greater than themselves. But let us examine this universal principle in more personal terms.

TRUE LOVERS LOSE THEMSELVES

A small baby is very self-centered. His world revolves around his own ego. He can't do very much for anyone else except smile, gurgle, and take his bottle when it is offered. Babies are just naturally egoists.

It requires a long while to grow up from self-centered babyhood. Some people never do. A good many teen-agers are still largely absorbed in themselves. The boy or girl at that age is likely to think of father and mother as being there just to give the youngster what he wants.

Of course, if he has been growing up at all, he has begun to have friends whom he cares about for their own sake. He has begun to feel sympathy (at least at times). He has had moments of generosity and thoughtfulness.

But when a boy falls in love he suddenly comes out of himself into something greater than himself. This girl he loves has swung open the gateways of life to new and wonderful experiences. Her loving him becomes one of the most marvelous facts of life. If he loves her truly, her happiness shines out as utterly important to him. And, of course, much the same thing happens to the girl when she falls truly in love.

The great word is no longer "I" but "we,"

no longer "mine" but "ours"

If these young lovers have begun to be at all mature, they begin to dream dreams of a future which grows up around the beloved. Our love, our purposes, our hopes, our future home, our children that are to be—these are the dreams that spring up first in sheer imagination, and then are worked out bit by bit through toil, struggle, aspiration, and love until they become the concrete realities of married life. The lovers have found themselves by losing themselves in something greater than themselves.

Suppose you were to go to a person who had been passing through the growing experience of true love, and suppose you were to ask him or her: "Isn't it a terrible sacrifice that you have to give up your 'I-self' in order to become part of this 'we-self'?" The lover would look at you in amazement. "No!"

he might exclaim. "Anything that was good and worthwhile in me before I met my beloved is still there—better and finer than ever. Anything which I brought into this relationship has been built up and glorified because we two have found love together."

Some projects are great; some small

Give yourself wholeheartedly to one, or two, or three great life projects, if you would live life to the full, richly and abundantly. Earlier in this chapter we listed five of these life-possessing projects—a career, marriage, parenthood, artistic creation, and the all-encompassing spiritual adventure.

Of course, many smaller projects may contribute toward the abundant life. To make a garden, to be a big brother to a boy who may thus be saved from becoming a criminal, to take a part in a play, to write a magazine or newspaper article (or even a letter to the editor) to sing in a choir, to teach a Sunday School class, to create a painting, to enter into and fulfill a friendship—the list could be extended indefinitely. Every such project has in it, in only lesser degree, a potential contribution toward fulfillment of life.

But what makes any one of these projects a life-fulfilling undertaking? To fulfill life thus, to bring joy now and growing joy in the future

A PROJECT MUST HAVE THREE CHARACTERISTICS

Let us look at these briefly.

1. To fulfill life, your project must keep rousing your energy

The first requirement for a life-fulfilling project is that it must call for the deepest and most powerful energies of your personality. It must rouse and quicken your body. It must stir your blood. It must be able to bring out the physical vigor of your muscles, your heart, your glands, and your nerves. It must challenge you so deeply that you are eager to devote your money and your other material resources to its achievement. It must stir your mind and your imagination, summoning and quickening your psychological urges. It must activate and set ablaze social relationships with your comrades, partners and associates in the project. And, to be fulfilling ultimately, this project must rouse into vivid intensity your spiritual energies.

This is one great reason why true love provides such a wonderful project for fulfillment of life. True love stirs some of the deepest and most powerful drives of the male and the female bodies. It calls out energy to work, to save money, to build a home, and to do other creative things with material objects. It stirs the mind. True lovers find that they have a vast number of things to talk about and to think about together. They quicken each other's intelligence. Each finds that he is a better person when they are together. And true love is one of the greatest ways of entering into spiritual experience, for in the depth of devotion between a man and a woman, they are each likely to discover something about the meaning of the love of God.

So, too, with a man's work. It must rouse his bodily energy—not merely now and then, or for a little while, but persistently, day after day, month after month, year after year, decade after decade. It must spur him to toil, creating material wealth. It must quicken his mind and stir his intelligence. It must waken and strengthen his friendships, his partnerships, and his capacity for teamwork. And it must stir harmonious power in his spiritual life. Thousands of years ago the ancients had a saying: "To labor is to pray."

Therefore, unless a project has this capacity to call forth your energy day after day, and year after year, it is not fit to be the object of your life's devotion. To live enthusiastically is one of the secrets of overflowing joy. In order that the enthusiastic life may be possible for you, make sure that you select a life partner, a life career, and your other projects with such care and insight that you can give yourself wholeheartedly and singlemindedly to them throughout the best years of your life.

2. To fulfill your life, your project must be creative

To plan to murder someone would be a project. But it would be destructive, not creative. Therefore it would wreck life instead of fulfilling it.

Getting rich by ruining other people could also be a project. But this also would be destructive more than creative. It, too, would wreck life instead of fulfilling it.

A Hitler, a Stalin, a gangster, a burglar, an embezzler—each of these is engaged in a project. But each of these is destroying, not fulfilling his own life and the life of others. Destructive projects lead down into hell-on-earth instead of up into heaven.

But true love is one of the most creative energies in the world. To take marriage and parenthood as your life project means giving yourself to creating a home, bringing children into the world, bringing into existence a center in which friendship, fellowship, and community service will flourish, and adding to the beauty and joy in your small part of the world. Therefore, on this second count also, these are among the greatest projects through which life can find fulfillment.

So, too, if you devote your life to being a doctor who is loyal to the Hippocratic oath or to the modern ethical code of the profession, if you become an enthusiastic worker in an enterprise that manufactures articles needed to create comfort, health, and well-being for your fellow human beings; or if you undertake any other life work which renders real service in the economic and social life of the nation and of the world, your career also has this second basic requirement for a life-fulfilling project.

3. Difficulties and hardships are essential

When Shakespeare wrote *Romeo and Juliet*, he, as author of the play, was the creator of the characters and of the lives that they lived in that drama. As far as the lives of those characters were concerned, Shakespeare was God. He had the power of good and evil and of life and death over them.

Why, then, did Shakespeare bring such frustration, grief, suffering, and tragedy to these two lovers? Since he had the power to make their lives just what he wanted them to be, why did he not set up a situation in which Romeo's family dearly loved Juliet's, and where both families were delighted when they learned that the young people were thinking about getting married? Why didn't Shakespeare arrange to have Romeo's family provide the young couple with a suitable mansion on a wonderful estate, and have Juliet's family provide a houseful of servants and an inexhaustible income for the young couple? Why didn't Shakespeare exercise his miracle-working power, as author, to see to it that they had four beautiful children, quite painlessly, that none of the children ever cried in the night or misbehaved in any way, and that they all grew up to be obedient, healthy, and successful?

If you are a young man, seeing a truly effective dramatization of this play, you will be caught up in the drama; you will, for the moment, be Romeo kissing Juliet. Or, if you are a young woman witnessing the same play, you for the moment will be Juliet, being kissed by Romeo. Thus a great dramatist makes it possible for those who witness his plays to live life through his characters. Why, then, did Shakespeare make you, as spectator of this play, participate in the grief, blundering, agony, and suicide of these young lovers? It is because the very essence of a good play is dramatic experience. And dramatic experience is not likely to come alive unless the play provides hazards, and at least some suffering.

Every good project has to have difficulties in it. In order to bring joy and fulfillment of life a project must have hardships, obstacles, suffering, and even the chance of failure. What is the fun in a football game if the score comes out 100 to 0? What is the fun in a baseball game if one team gets a dozen runs each inning and the other team gets none at all?

But once this requirement is stated, it becomes clear that

marriage, parenthood, and one's life work all involve difficulties, dangers, hardships, suffering, and possible failure. These are necessary to a good project. When we realize this, we will have a new understanding of the "problem of evil" in the world.

THE SPIRITUAL LIFE AS THE
SUPREME PROJECT

Let's suppose that long ago, before you were even born, you were standing with the Supreme Dramatist, communing with Him about the life which you were about to live on earth. Let us suppose that the Supreme Dramatist spoke to you somewhat as follows:

> Down on that little earth which you see spinning there in the solar system I am producing a stupendous drama. If you decide to do so, you are to have a part in that drama. Do you consent?

And then you answered eagerly:

> Oh, yes, Master! It will be wonderful to have any part in the drama which You are creating on Earth.

But then the Dramatist looked at you searchingly and said:

> Wait a minute! Before you accept, you must know that you yourself will have to compose your lines in the play as you go along. You yourself will create your part in the plot; you will bring into being the character which you are to play. Are you willing to attempt that?

And then you said, rather hesitantly:

> Well, Master, I am very ignorant and I am not brilliant. I suppose that when I start on this play I shall be a bewildered little baby. Perhaps I'll mess things up. Perhaps I'll spoil your play by my blundering and my shortsightedness.

Then the Master went on:

That risk is part of the drama. The play is being given so that you, and all your fellow human beings can learn to live the spiritual life. Here is your chance to learn to live lovingly. Here is your opportunity to learn to know Me through your life with other struggling and searching human beings.

But there is one other thing you need to know before you make your choice. In this play there will be moments of high joy, achievement, and vision. But there will also be much suffering, many defeats, much of hardships and sometimes of terror. You will be in the midst of it. And most of the time you will have forgotten that it is only a play. You will feel that it is terribly real, that all your destiny it at stake, and sometimes that utter disaster may be crashing in upon you.

Then you said:

I am not sure that I want to do that, Master. If the play is likely to be a tragedy, with utter grief and ruin at the end, I'd rather stay here with You and not go down into the murk and the muck and the blood and the tears.

Then the Supreme Dramatist said to you:

It shall be as you decide. But know this. In the midst of the struggle and the pain and the danger, if you look up with seeking heart and searching eye you will catch glimpses of Me. You will hear echoes of angels' songs. You will find courage and faith surging up in your heart when you truly pray.

And at long last, when you have finished your part on the stage of life, and said your last line, you will go out into the wings, and lay off your costume, and rub off your make-up, and come out joyously into a wider world overarched with stars.

So here you are. Do you remember?

Chapter 3

Take God Into Your Adventure

THESE ARE INESCAPABLE FACTS

Something in you thinks "I": Where did it come from?

Within your body, something thinks "I." This "I" probably seems to you to be located somewhere back of your eyes and between your ears.

Now, whatever it is that thinks "I" in you came from somewhere. You can remember back along a chain of experiences. Those memories go back into your childhood. What was the source of this "I"?

You are now, at this moment, using something which you call "my body." Before you were born, that body was part of your mother's body. Before your mother was born, she was part of your grandmother's body. Before your grandmother was born, she was part of your great-grandmother's body. So we must all admit that these physical bodies of ours are part of the vast chain of life, which encircles this globe and which stretches back into the past, for ages which scientists measure in hundreds of millions of years.

This tells us something which cannot be denied. Conscious-

24

ness is born out of this Universe of ours. Out of its surging forces there arises something which thinks "I" in each of billions of human beings. If you have a pet dog, you feel sure that he too is conscious. So are our horses, our birds, and our other pets. So even are wild animals.

Your body has energy flowing through it

When you are rested and healthy, you are energetic. Where does that energy come from? Through all your life, three times a day (more or less) you have been eating food. The chemists and the doctors who know about these things tell us that our bodily energy comes from digesting that food. But where did the food get its energy? Originally, that energy came from the sun. Out across the wheatfields, the pasture lands, the banana plantations, the coffee plantations, and all across the other places from which our food has come, the sun has been pouring down energy which plants and animals have taken in. When we ate our bread or our egg, or drank our milk, or put sugar in our coffee, we were laying hold of the energy that streams out from the sun. And the sun is a raging furnace that pours forth the energy of the Universe. We can call it "cosmic energy."

Here is a strange fact, full of deep meaning. This cosmic energy can be transformed. Sun-power drinks up water from the oceans and from the surface of the earth. It lifts the water into the sky, and lets it fall on mountains. Then dynamos, at hydroelectric plants, turn this stored-up cosmic energy into a current that flows through copper wires. When men tap that current and run it through electric bulbs or tubes, the power shines out in the form of *light*.

In the wheatfield, in the cow, and in our own bodies, that very same cosmic energy comes alive. When we take that energy in our bread or in our milk, and when the chemical plant that we call our stomach turns it into a form which our nerves can use, that energy can flow into our brains and can there light up in the form of *consciousness*. You can sum it up in one sentence: "We do our thinking by means of the very same energy which runs the Universe!"

"IN HIM WE LIVE, AND MOVE, AND HAVE OUR BEING"

The scientific fact is inescapable that we do our thinking with the energy which runs the Cosmos. But is that cosmic energy alive? Does HE think? Nineteen centuries ago, that question (in a somewhat different form) was put to the traveling preacher Paul, the Apostle—that same Paul whose letters are such an important part of the New Testament. Some philosophers, who had been disputing in Athens, set Paul up on the Hill of Mars and he delivered an address which interpreted the above scientific fact in this form:

> The God who made the world and all things in it, He, as Lord of heaven and earth, does not dwell in shrines that are made by human hands; He is not served by human hands as if He needed anything, for it is He who gives life, and breath and all things to all men. All nations He has created from a common origin, to dwell all over the earth, fixing their allotted periods and the boundaries of their abodes, meaning them to seek for God on the chance of finding Him in their groping for Him. Though indeed He is close to each one of us, for it is in Him that we live and move and exist.

Is the Cosmos "He" or "it"?

Paul said: "In *Him* we live, and move, and exist." Science tells us that cosmic energy lights up in our brains in the form of thought. But does the Cosmos itself think? For thousands of years the philosophers have been arguing about that question.

Here is one way to seek light on it. Relax deeply and then read to yourself out loud, one sentence at a time, the following passage, pausing after each sentence to ask yourself: "What does this mean? Is it true or is it false?"

> "I am not my body; I am that which uses my body.
> "I am not my emotions; I am that which controls my emotions.
> "I am not my thoughts; I am that which directs my thoughts.
> "I am a spirit!
> "God is a spirit; and they that worship Him must worship Him in spirit and in truth.
> "Speak to Him, thou, for He answers, and spirit with spirit can meet. Nearer is He than breathing, closer than hands or feet."

As I am to my body, so God is to the universe. We cannot prove that. But what more plausible theory has anyone to offer?

All through the ages the seers and seekers, the prophets and the saints, have testified that they *know* God in the same way that they know themselves. With a deep, powerful certainty, they have experienced their oneness with the Eternal.

If we, then, are willing to make the venture of faith, if we are willing to test out the belief that the universe has in it a Supreme Conscious Self, in Whom we live and move and exist, and Who responds to our deepest needs and our highest aspirations, then the rational and reasonable thing to do is to reach out and to seek to make contact with that Supreme Being. That reaching out, that seeking to establish working relations with spiritual reality, is what is meant by prayer.

SIX STEPS TO GOD

To adventure spiritually does not mean to accept blindly any dogma, or even any creed. Every explorer seeks to find out more about Reality. If by any chance, He Who created us meant for us to seek Him, on the chance of finding Him in our groping, let us at least reach out and test the hypothesis that God is there. This reaching out can take the form of the following six steps:

1. Give God opportunities to talk to you

Most people, when they pray, spend all their time talking at God. They tell him what they want and how they feel. But if we seriously propose to make the venture of faith, what we need to do is to tune in on God. Long centuries before the time of Jesus it was written: "Be still and know that I am God." Learning to pray is a vital step in taking God into our adventure. We shall think it through much more deeply later on.

2. Purge out the obstacles

The ancient Hebrew prophet Elijah, who was trying to run away, came out from his cave after the wind, and the earthquake, and the fire. Then he heard God speaking in "a still, small voice." Holy men of the East have called it "the Voice of Silence." Quakers have found the Will of God through "the Inner Light." But how shall we hear that Voice if our ears are filled with the tumult of the market place and the factory? How shall we hear it above the shouted demands of desires which we know must be out of harmony with any high and holy Purpose? How shall we see the Inner Light if our gaze is wholly occupied with greedy and angry visions?

3. Act on the guidance that God gives you

Listening prayer brings guidance in our perplexities. God's inspiration is found to be available when we seek it. Be not disobedient to the heavenly vision! Acting on inspiration brings the reward of further inspiration. Refusing to follow the Light means that the Light is likely to be withdrawn.

4. Bring God's courage into your daily living

If God really loves you, there is absolutely nothing in the world to be afraid of. He is your sure defense. He gives the strength to triumph over all your troubles. "Be of good courage, and He will strengthen your heart. Wait, I say, on the Lord."

5. Don't ask God to take away all hardship, suffering, danger, and defeat

Life itself can be a magnificent adventure. You and I want to live life to the full. We don't want to be packed in cotton wool and raised in a hothouse. Others have been heroic. Others have faced danger, difficulty, and even defeat. How tame, and insipid, and pointless life would be if there were no problems to solve, no difficulties to overcome, no victories to be won. As Browning put it:

"Let me fare like my peers, the heroes of old."

But when we take faith into the battle we take also courage. We are testing the hypothesis that Divine Leadership can be ours. Empowered by that faith, difficulties turn into achievements.

6. Pass on to others the discoveries of God that come to you

Those who are spiritually enlightened become links in a vast chain leading from Earth up to the very Throne of God. Each living link holds one hand upward to clasp the hand of an elder brother—the leader, teacher, guide, whom God has sent to show the next step and to give the strength to take that step. But each link also reaches the other hand downward to clasp that of the little brother who needs help. Every enlightened person becomes a chela, a pupil who seeks and finds spiritual guidance and help. And every spiritually enlightened person becomes a guru, a teacher and leader who transmits spiritual power to others who are in need of it. It is in this transmitting process that we become truly alive in spirit. Only he who teaches can most fully learn. Only he who helps can truly be helped.

HERE, THEN, ARE THE STEPS IN OUR INITIAL SEARCH FOR GOD

This chapter is only a brief sketch of steps that we must follow if we seek to take God into our spiritual adventure. But it may be of help to sum these up still more briefly, as in the following:

1. Among the inescapable facts are these:

> **You are conscious.**
> **Your body is a channel through which energy flows.**
> **In your brain, cosmic energy lights up in the form of consciousness.**

2. "In Him we live, and move, and exist" was Paul's interpretation of the above facts.

> **One way to think of it is this: "As I am to my body, so God is to the universe."**

3. We can adventure spiritually by taking six steps:

> **Give God opportunities to talk to you.**
> **Purge out the obstacles.**
> **Act on the guidance that God gives you.**
> **Bring God's courage into your daily living.**
> **Don't ask God to take away all hardship.**
> **Pass on to others the discoveries of God which come to you.**

⬛⬛⬛⬛⬛⬛⬛⬛⬛⬛⬛⬛⬛⬛⬛⬛⬛⬛⬛⬛⬛⬛⬛⬛⬛⬛⬛⬛⬛⬛⬛⬛

Chapter 4

We Die—Then What?

This is an old, old problem

More than two thousand years ago, Job asked his friends: "If a man die, shall he live again?" The hope of immortality is, indeed, far older than that. A skeleton has been found which was laid to rest more than 50,000 years ago. When that body was buried, gifts were buried with it. Those who loved that prehistoric man hoped and believed that his spirit lived on beyond the grave.

How can we find a true answer to Job's question? How can we prove whether the "I" goes on living, loving and growing beyond physical death?

CHRISTIANITY WAS BASED ON PSYCHIC PHENOMENA

Otherwise Christianity could not have gotten started

Passage after passage can be cited from the New Testament in which accounts of psychic phenomena are presented as basic to the Christian religion. One of the most striking passages of this sort is contained in the fifteenth chapter of Paul's first letter to the Corinthians, of which an abridged version is as follows:

> I passed on to you what I had myself received, namely, that Christ died, and that he was buried, that he rose on the third day, and that he was seen by Cephas, then by the Twelve; and that he was seen by over five hundred brothers all at once, the majority of whom have survived to this day; after that he was seen by James, then by all the apostles, and finally he was seen by myself.
>
> If dead men never rise, Christ did not rise either; and if Christ did not rise, your faith is futile.
>
> But it is not so! Christ did rise from the dead.
>
> But someone will ask, "How do the dead rise? What kind of body have they when they come?" Foolish man! What you sow never comes to life unless it dies. What is sown is mortal, what rises is immortal; sown inglorious, it rises in glory; sown in weakness, it rises in power; sown an animate body, it rises a spiritual body. As there is an animate body, so there is a spiritual body.

The above passage is a particularly striking document in view of the fact that close to the end of this letter we find the words:

"I, Paul, write this salutation with my own hand."

Here, then, we have a document of which the original was endorsed by Paul himself, and in which he transmits the testimony of witnesses who reported six different appearances of Jesus after his resurrection. Paul himself had talked with many of these witnesses.

Modern evidence confirms it

This is not the place to review even samples of the vast collection of case records which confirm this fact. But such events have occurred so persistently, in all the leading countries of the world, that learned societies have been created to study psychical phenomena in England, in the United States, in South America, in continental European countries, and even in Asia and Africa. Down through the ages, persistent voices have kept calling to mankind, urging that in the midst of our struggles to make a living in this material world we lift up our eyes and become aware of the infinite spiritual realities that surround us.

BELIEF IN LIFE BEYOND DEATH IS RATIONAL

Skeptics kept raising doubts

Hundreds of years before the time of Christ, Job's "Comforters" asked skeptical questions about life beyond death. In the passage quoted above from Paul's letter to the Corinthians, he cites the doubters of that day ("But someone will ask, 'How do the dead rise? What kind of body have they when they come?' Foolish man! . . .") Strikingly similar is the question that one of America's leading psychologists, Dr. Gardner Murphy, raised in an article that was published in the *Journal of the American Society for Psychical Research* for July, 1945, where he remarked: "There are difficulties in imagining what a 'personal existence' would be like without a [physical] body. . . ."

Many others have kept asking questions such as these: "If there are worlds beyond the grave, where are they located? Is heaven 'up in the sky?' Is hell 'down below?' "

These came back from beyond death

Shakespeare's Hamlet refers to the land beyond the grave as "the undiscover'd country, from whose bourn no traveler returns." But various travelers into the regions beyond the grave *have* returned, and have told of their experiences. In England, a distinguished scientist, Dr. Robert Crookall, has made it his avocation to collect such records, together with accounts of several kinds of closely related phenomena. From cases in his collection the following summaries have been taken:

> George Kelley, M.D., had been pronounced dead by his medical attendant. Subsequently he recovered and related to his wife the following experience. He went through a momentary darkness, a void. Then he saw his sister-in-law, who had preceded him through the gates of death some years before, but who had not returned to her physical body. Dr. Kelley then turned to his grieving wife and tried to tell her that he was not dead but very much alive, more alive than ever he had been during his earth life. She could not hear him. He touched her but she failed to respond to his touch. He knew that she thought that he still occupied that inert body which was lying on the bed.
>
> He then felt a sudden swift movement away from his physical body. He felt on the very verge of "another existence [one] entirely different from that of earth." He told his wife later: "I was experiencing what is known as death, but what, in reality, is transition. . . . I realized that death is no longer a thing of fear. . . . The knowledge I gained at that time assured me of the future life."

Mrs. Frances Leslie had a similar experience. She had been pronounced dead, but on being given an injection, she revived. She then told of having seemed to herself to be floating in a long tunnel. When she emerged she found herself separated from her physical body and occupying a second "astral" or "etheric" body, which floated in the air defying all the laws of gravity. When the injection forced her to return, she did so with reluctance; an expression of sadness escaped from her. But her return was only temporary; twelve hours later she left her physical body permanently.

In 1937, Sir Aucland Geddes reported to the Royal Medical Society of Edinburgh the experiences of a doctor friend who was at the point of death. This friend told of having left his physical body, which he could see lying on the bed. He found himself in a luminous and non-physical body. In that state he found himself clairvoyant; he was able to see what was transpiring in London, in Scotland, and, indeed, wherever he turned his attention. Sir Aucland concluded his narrative thus:

> What are we to make of it? Of one thing only we can be quite sure—it was not a fake. Without that certainty I should not have brought it to your notice.

Like several of the above, Elizabeth Bleakley died but recovered. Her experience is recounted in *Prediction,* for March, 1953. When she left her physical body she experienced a momentary blackout. Then she found herself floating up above, looking down upon her corpse. She thought: "This is death!" After her return she was utterly convinced that the soul survives the death of the body; to her the matter was now "beyond intellectual doubt."

Philosophers have shown that survival is rational

One of the leading philosophers in America is Professor C. J. Ducasse, recently retired as head of the Philosophy Department at Brown University. He published a massive tome in 1951, called *Nature, Mind, and Death.* In that book he exposed the fallacies of the philosophers who have claimed that belief in life beyond death is irrational. One of the leading philosophers of Great Britain, Professor H. H. Price, of Oxford University, reviewed Professor Ducasse's book, and expressed fundamental agreement with much of what is set forth there.

Scientific evidence confirms the philosophers

That life beyond death is logically conceivable seems clear from the conclusions of Professor Ducasse and Professor Price. But theories always have to be tested in terms of data. We need *cases.* To collect such cases, and to study them, a group of distinguished leaders of British thought founded the Society for Psychical Research in England, in 1882. Since then, for more than three-quarters of a century, not only in England but also in the United States and in many other countries, scientific researchers, with critical keenness, have been examining vast volumes of evidence. In 1956, a group of outstanding investigators in this field brought together nearly 200 evidentially tested cases, analyzed them searchingly both by logic and by statistics, and published their findings in a treatise called "Six Theories About Apparitions." Very briefly, the conclusions of that study may be summed up in the following propositions:

1. "Ghosts" are objective realities

Apparitions, not only of the dead and the dying but also of living persons, have been observed and recorded by so many different people, in so many different places, at so many different times, and the observations reported are so consistent with one another, that only the stubborn and uninformed skeptic can conceal from himself the fact that such phenomena are real.

2. Such apparitions have been observed collectively

They have not only been seen by single individuals; in many cases they have been observed by two or more people at the same time, and what each of the observers sees is consistent with and verifies what each of the other observers sees.

For example, in June, 1931, Samuel Bull died of cancer in Ramsbury, Wilts., England. Eight months later, for about seven weeks during the spring of 1932, the apparition of this "dead" man was seen repeatedly by his widow, his married daughter, his son-in-law, and his grandchildren. In one case all nine members of the family together saw the apparition. Whenever it was seen, all the persons present were able to see it. The apparition seemed solid; twice he is reported to have laid his hand on the brow of his widow. Once she heard him call her "Jane." Once the figure was visible continuously for a half hour. It always appeared to be quite lifelike. The features were clearly recognized. He was dressed as he usually had been in the evenings when he had finished work.

Such appearances cannot be figments of the individuals' imaginations. They are objective realities, jointly and collectively perceived by independent observers.

3. Some living persons have left their bodies temporarily

Apparitions of the living, in a number of well-authenticated cases, have been vehicles within which the consciousness of the appearing person actually observed what was going on, acted out his purposes and even spoke his thoughts, and later remembered the experience and was able to check his observations against those of other witnesses.

4. Some apparitions of the dead are conscious

That the conscious apparitions of the living are the same basic kind of phenomenon as apparitions of the dead, has been demonstrated quite conclusively by statistics as well as by logical investigation.

Personal survival is the only adequate deduction

Apparently then, since apparitions of the living can be vehicles in which conscious personalities observe and act at distances away from their physical bodies, and since apparitions of the dying and the dead have been demonstrated to be the same essential kind of phenomenon, giving similar evidences of purpose, of continuing love, of adjustment to environment, and of interaction with the observer, the only sound conclusion would seem to be that apparitions of those who have permanently left their physical bodies are also vehicles of continuing personal consciousness and identity. In other words, human personality does survive bodily death.

A BRITISH SCHOLAR REPORTED HIS VISITS TO THE OTHER WORLD

Many cases could be cited of people who have "died," and who, after their bodies were brought back to life, remembered experiences in which they made contact with loved ones who had previously passed on beyond the grave. In the limited space available here, it may be illuminating to cite briefly some experiences of a distinguished British scholar, John S. M. Ward, a contributor to the *Encyclopedia Britannica,* whose achievements have been listed at length in the British *Who's Who.*

It started with a precognitive vision

Early in December, 1913, Mr. Ward had a vision which began with a message that his uncle (who was also the father of Mr. Ward's wife, Carrie) had died. In the vision, Mr. Ward found himself at the funeral. The sensations of grief, and the remarks and actions of the other mourners, were vividly impressed on his mind. When he awoke he told his wife about the vision.

On January 5th the death actually occurred. All the sensations of grief that Mr. Ward had felt in his dream were repeated, and so were the detailed incidents of the funeral.

His "dead" uncle conducted him

During the night of January 12th, Mr. Ward dreamed that he saw his uncle, who gave him the following message:

> I have been trying to speak to Carrie, but can't, so I have come to you. Tell her I am alive, more alive than before I died; that I am mentally clearer than I was for some time before I died. But here I have set to work to learn, as if I were a child again, much of what I should have learned on earth. . . .

This began a long series of weekly visions, in which Mr. Ward's uncle took him away from his physical body into the regions beyond the grave, and showed him in great detail what life there was like. Mr. Ward published a series of books in which he reported these experiences.

The testimony piles up

Scores of other books have been published by people who sincerely and earnestly believe that they also have received definite and clear information about the conditions of life beyond the grave. In some details, these books appear to contradict each other. This is due to the fact that the life beyond death is lived in a mental world, where conditions in many ways are basically different from those to which we are accustomed here in our physical bodies and our material surroundings. The kind of world in which the surviving spirit finds himself depends essentially on the kind of ideas, aspirations, prejudices, hopes, spiritual insights and social relationships which he developed while he was still living in his physical body. But when we take full account of that basic fact, the underlying and fundamental harmonies between the various reports of the afterlife begin to come clear.

WHAT LIFE BEYOND DEATH IS SAID TO BE LIKE

What we propose to do here is to explore the survival hypothesis, so as to find out what its full acceptance would mean. We propose also to explore how you and I can adjust our lives and our personalities so as to live joyously and creatively, both while in the physical body and also beyond the gates of death.

The evidence collected by systematic and critical research, during the past three-quarters of a century, indicates that the spiritual universe has vast and magnificent regions which lie beyond the boundaries of this material world, and beyond the reach of our bodily senses. Moreover, the accumulated evidence has developed clear outlines of the experiences that we are likely to encounter "when we have shuffled off this mortal coil," and of the conditions upon which our joy or our misery in that afterlife will most probably depend.

Obviously, there must be many things about even the first stages of the life beyond death which we do not understand in our normal waking consciousness, here in our physical

bodies. Still more, this must be true about the spiritual regions which (according to our working hypothesis) stretch onward and upward beyond the simpler, nearby stages. But there
are a few fundamentals that seem to stand out in all the leading accounts of the future life, and that appear to be logical,
once one has accepted the facts established by psychical research. On the basis of voluminous evidence and believable
reports, the following may be taken (at least tentatively) as the
basic facts as to what our experiences at and after death are
likely to be like.

The experience of dying

There are as many different ways of dying as there are people who die. But the great majority of deaths are said to have
certain common features, which may be summed up as follows:
When your physical body dies, you will find yourself very
much alive, and occupying a body that seems to you to be just
as real and solid as was the body that you have left behind.
You are likely to find yourself in the company of others who
seem to know what is happening, and who are welcoming and
helping you make your first adjustments to this new life. Among
these welcomers are likely to be some whom you "have loved
long since, and lost a while," dear ones of yours who have pre-
ceded you through the gates of death. These loved ones and
wise guides will encourage you to leave behind your physical
remains and the place where you have died. Under their care,
you will sink into a sleep that (in terms of earthly time) is
likely to last several days.

Beyond death are various regions

The immense variety of the realms beyond the grave is testified to with much unanimity. Jesus himself said: "In my
father's house are many mansions." And Moses is reported, in
Deuteronomy, to have mentioned "the lowest Hell" in his song
to the assembly of Israel. Modern explorers of the realms beyond death are even more specific.

The earth-bound region

Many of those who leave their physical bodies for the last time find themselves held by the habits of their past earth life, and by their lack of understanding of the nature of the life beyond death. Such a one is likely, at first, to be unable to get away from the old familiar haunts in which he used to live, work, and play. Yet he also finds himself unable, beyond death, to reestablish his normal life, because he usually cannot make his former friends see or hear him; he cannot normally open or close a door, eat physical food, write on a sheet of paper or a blackboard, nor do any of the physical acts that would make his presence known or that would make it possible for him to enter with any real effect into the life from which his physical body has departed. Dr. Robert Crookall believes that a temporary earthbound condition is particularly likely to be true of persons who have died in the prime of life, through accidents, war, or disease.

Those who have departed earth

Beyond the earthbound zone there are spiritual areas in which no physical bodies of human beings, and no physical objects of earth are present. Many "astral projectors" report that they have visited these regions. Two kinds of spirits are found in these beyond-earth planes. Here are "the dead"—those who have permanently left their physical bodies behind, and here are some who are projected while their physical bodies sleep. Some of these, after awaking, may remember fragments of such experiences as if they had been dreams.

In these beyond-earth regions, thoughts are things. In any given area of these planes, the inhabitants find themselves surrounded by the kinds of landscapes, dwellings, work-places and other objects that are normally created by their own shared memories, imaginations, aspirations, hopes and fears. The processes by which these surroundings are created may be regarded

as being similar to the processes by which shared dreams come
into being.

Spiritual gravitation

In this realm of the afterlife, like seeks like. The inhabitants of any given area are selected by character-attraction.
Birds of a feather flock together. When we leave our mortal
bodies and pass beyond the earth-bound region, we gravitate
inevitably into the company of the kind of people whose com-
panionship we have earned by the kind of life we have lived,
the kinds of thoughts we have been thinking, and the kinds of
values we have cherished.

Al Capone's Hell

What happens after death may be illustrated by asking ourselves what must have been the experiences of two famous
American characters when they finally left their mortal bodies.
One of these was Al Capone, a gangster who is reputed to have
been responsible for retail and wholesale murders, for corrupt-
ing police, and for extorting money from innocent people by
vicious threats. His gang is reported to have controlled gambling, prostitution, and bootleg liquor in areas around Chicago. While spending seven years in a Federal penitentiary
(for tax evasion!), he developed a syphilitic infection of the
brain. He died in 1947.

Since he had lived 48 years (more than half of the normal
span of the human life on earth) we may assume that his stay
in the earth regions after death was relatively brief. When he
finally became conscious in the regions to which his earthly
life had destined him, spiritual gravitation would result in his
finding himself in the midst of gangsters like himself, in the
kind of surroundings which the memories and imagination of
such people would naturally create. That is to say, he would
be surrounded by spirits who had built up in themselves the

habits of trying to impose their wills on others by fear, force, and fraud. He would be in the company of men who were trying to gain power by terrorizing others, by deceiving them, and by exerting physical violence against them. He would be associated with women who were in the habit of seeking power by ruthless use of their own physical attractions, and by imitating the gun play, the violence and the treachery of their men associates. He might find himself in places having something of the glitter of the underworld to which he had been accustomed, but always under the pressures of fear, force, and fraud.

Furthermore, Al Capone would find himself in the presence of the victims whose lives he had helped to wreck through his gangster activities—people whom he had murdered, the widows and orphans of his victims, people whose lives he had helped to make miserable by his threats of extortion, public officials whom he had helped to pull down into degradation by his bribes and threats, and women whom he had helped to force and to trick into lives of ill-fame. All those who had come to hate and despise him would be drawn to him in the afterlife by spiritual gravitation. If any of his victims had freed themselves from these shackles of hate and fear, dream forms representing them would still crowd in upon Al Capone and menace him.

Wouldn't that be hell! That sentence might at first seem to be profane. Actually, it is not, because Al Capone would (under this hypothesis) find himself in a hell that he himself had helped to create, and to which he had destined himself, by the kind of earthly life which he had lived.

Jane Addams' Heaven

In contrast with the after-death experience of the gangster, let us consider what would happen (under this theory) to anyone distinguished for loving comradeship and service to his or her fellowmen. For example, let us think what may presumably have happened to the great American social worker, Jane Addams.

From childhood, Miss Addams had been eager to make life richer for the underprivileged. When she graduated from college, her physician prescribed a trip abroad. She went to Russia and sat at the feet of Tolstoy, the world-famous apostle of peace. She went to London, and visited Toynbee Hall, a social settlement created in the spirit of a man who had given his life in the effort to enrich the lives of working people.

When Miss Addams returned to America, she purchased the old Hull mansion on Halsted Street in Chicago, in a region where tenements and slums had been crowding in. She never married; she spent the rest of her life in Hull House, being a good neighbor to immigrants, factory workers, mothers and fathers who were trying to rear healthy children in the slums, and young people who were trying to grow up into healthy and joyous manhood and womanhood in spite of the handicaps of the tenement-house district.

When Jane Addams died, after a long life rich in social service, she too (under our hypothesis) would find herself among spirits of her own kind, in surroundings such as would be created by the aspirations and ideals of such people. Countless persons to whom she had given loving service and friendly help would be waiting eagerly to greet her. She would be surrounded by the kind of people who tried enthusiastically to create beauty in their homes, who cared for handicrafts, literature, drama, art, and music, and who had formed the lifelong habit of working together for the common good. She would find herself in a region of lovely homes, beautiful gardens, magnificent public buildings, and wide sweeping vistas of country life. Wouldn't that be heavenly! It *would* be heaven, because people like Jane Addams create heaven for themselves and their associates by the way they have lived on earth. Heaven is a social state in which all freely and joyously work together for the common good.

Beyond the earth-like regions lie infinite realms of

spiritual growth

Although the accounts of life beyond death are virtually unanimous in telling about the regions in which cooperative thinking creates visible and tangible surroundings that may be beautiful, friendly, and developing, such accounts also agree that beyond the earth-like regions lie realms of spiritual growth that cannot readily be explained in terms of our sensory experiences in the material world. We get intimations of such a life in terms of our earthly experiences of beauty in music, and in poetry. Abstract thinking in science and philosophy also provides clues for the spiritual realms that lie beyond the world of form. And, above all, the deepest and truest experiences of worship and of spiritual communion may provide the beginnings of awareness of these further regions of the spiritual world.

DEATH IS A GATEWAY TO LIFE MORE MAGNIFICENT

The most dreadful problems of life lose their dread if we grasp the true meaning of death. What of the young men whose lives have been cut short in battle? What of the mother who has seen her baby snatched away by a tragic accident? What of the young father who has watched his beloved pass away through the gates of death, just at the time when her mothering is needed desperately by their children? What of you or me, or someone near and dear to us, who may be called upon to endure the agony of fatal cancer? What of those who go down to death in loneliness and want? The list of such life-shattering problems might be lengthened, on and on.

But death is a gateway into a more magnificent life. Once we realize that, the anguish, the apparent defeat, the bereavement—all these become endurable and more and more understandable. Then, when we learn to use day by day the prayer that works wonders, we begin to find that we can walk through the valley of the shadow of death triumphantly.

WE DIE—THEN THIS

To the question raised in the title of this chapter, an answer has been offered. It is not a dogmatic answer. Rather it presents a working hypothesis about the nature of the life that awaits us beyond the gates of death. The essential points in this answer are summed up here.

Christianity was founded on psychic phenomena—it could not have got started without them. Ample modern evidence confirms the occurrence of after-death appearances.

Belief in life beyond death is rational. Eminent philosophers have shown the reasonableness of such a conception. Distinguished fiction writers have helped us to grasp the meaning of shared experiences that lie beyond this physical world.

To die is to leave one's physical body behind, but to go on in a body that is just as real, into a tangible and visible world where association is renewed with loved ones who have gone on before, and where the heavenly or hellish quality of experience is the direct and natural result of how one has lived on earth.

Beyond death are various regions—the earthbound, the earthlike of those who have departed earth, and the further regions of infinite spiritual growth. Spiritual gravitation produces hells like that of Al Capone, and heavens, like that of Jane Addams.

Death is a gateway to life more magnificent.

Book **II**

You Can Work Wonders

Through Prayer

Chapter *5*

These Lives Were Guided:

How About Yours?

All through the ages, innumerable groups have sought for spiritual guidance. The Hebrew prophets, the ancient Essenes, the Mithraists, Zen Buddhists, followers of Ignatius Loyola, Quakers, Buchmanites—the list might be extended almost without limit. The basic reason for this persistent search, throughout the ages, in all the countries of the world, is that spiritual guidance is real, and that to obtain it is of vital importance.

One of the most recent group endeavors to learn more about guidance, and to apply it more effectively in individual lives, is The Spiritual Frontiers Fellowship.* Its members live in 31 states, three Canadian provinces, Panama, and England. These people believe in spiritual guidance. Most of them believe in it because they themselves, over and over again, have experienced it. Others have joined the movement because they too want to experience it.

"Spiritual Guidance as a Scientific Problem" was the title

---

* The headquarters of the organization are at 1229 Hinman Avenue, Evanston, Illinois.

of the keynote address at a conference of this Fellowship, held in a suburb of Chicago in May, 1957. After that address more than 300 people signed cards, indicating their desire to collaborate in studying this problem. After the conference, the collaborating members were invited to send in written accounts of guidance experiences that they believed might prove to be helpful to others. The case stories that are summarized in this chapter are taken from the widespread returns which responded to that invitation.

FOUR STRIKING EXAMPLES COME FROM ONE GUIDED LIFE

All of the first four examples of this series took place in the experiences of a wife and mother, whom we will call Mrs. Gwynne Oliphant.

She was guided to marry the right husband

One of the most crucial decisions that any of us have to make is the one that leads to marriage—or to the breaking up of a relationship that might have led to marriage. A right decision here may lead on to rich fulfillment of life, in a home where love and shared purpose give strength, comfort, vision, and power to succeed. A wrong decision about marriage may be the blunder that plunges the mistaken couple into disillusionment, mutual damage, agonizing quarrels, divorce, and the wrecking of children's lives.

Is it right to pray for guidance in courtship problems? Gwynne believed that it was. That faith is what led to her becoming Mrs. Gwynne Oliphant. She has described this experience thus:

> Twenty-five years ago I was considering a proposal of marriage; the young man seemed desirable in every way, yet I did not feel sure he was right for me. But I thought this might be an unrealistic attitude on my part, and so was in great conflict. When pressed for a decision, I called inwardly for help in making the

right choice—and a clear and definite word filled my
mind: "Wait!" I did so, and a week later met the man
who became my husband in a supremely happy marriage.

Guidance led her to the right house for her family

To find the right habitation, within which to make a home
with your true love, is another problem that countless couples
have found perplexing. These people who have learned to seek
and to obtain a spiritual guidance tell us that solutions for
such problems come with a wisdom that reaches out beyond
any ordinary knowledge. This is what happened to Mrs. Oliphant's family when she used guidance to solve a problem of
that kind:

> Five years ago we had to move, under pressure of
> time, and had little opportunity for selecting the lo-
> cality or house. We chose a certain town, with some
> doubts, and could find there only two suitable houses,
> each with drawbacks. Under pressure, we had to give
> a quick decision and it seemed almost impossible to
> make. I asked, in prayer, for guidance, and immedi-
> ately these words came: "It does not matter which
> house you choose; the important thing is that you *are*
> to be in that town." I then felt a complete sense of
> peace about the whole matter; we went to our ap-
> pointment still not sure which house to decide upon,
> only to find that a third house had become available
> that was exactly right for us in every way!

Guidance solved her daughter's teen-age problem

The guided life encounters new problems as soon as marriage leads to parenthood. Mother and father have learned how
to reach out for superhuman enlightenment and strength. But
how is this spiritual knowledge to be transmitted to the children? The newspapers are full of tragic stories about how teen-
agers damage their own lives, and the lives of others, by mak-

ing wrong decisions at crucial moments. Most of this teen-age wreckage comes in families where the parents first made the basic failures. But all conscientious parents encounter crises in their children's lives, where the need for spiritual guidance becomes intense. Mrs. Oliphant gives us the following examples from her own life:

> Four years ago our daughter became involved in a teen-age romance which she thought we didn't know about and which required parental interference, but we were most anxious to deal with it carefully. It involved preventing a pre-arranged meeting, and we were at a loss as to how to do this wisely and as happily as possible for all concerned. Both my husband and I prayed for guidance as to what we should do. We both got the same answer: "Leave it alone; don't do anything, and it will all be taken care of." And it was—by an unexpected occurrence which prevented the meeting and broke off all contact.

Guidance delivered her from a crucial worry

Someone has said that everyone who marries and has children "gives hostages to fortune." To love means to risk the loss of the loved one. Brave people take that risk gladly, because of the joy that love releases. Spiritual guidance can safeguard that joy by providing faith and insight by which any emergency can be met with courage. Mrs. Oliphant gives the following example:

> Three years ago my husband suddenly became almost fatally ill while we were on a trip, and was rushed to the hospital in a strange city where we knew no one. The doctor warned me that he might not survive, and in a panic I cried out inwardly: "What shall I do? If I could just know the outcome—so I could prepare for it!" The answer clearly came: "He is going to be all right. It will take time, but he will be all right." And he was; he made a remarkable and full recovery,

after several weeks of convalescence, and the assurance
which I had received enabled me to go through the
crisis calmly and in confidence.

GUIDANCE SAVED HIS LIFE AND IMPROVED
HIS INVESTMENTS

W. Wipprecht, Jr., of Kendall, Florida, is a pilot with one
of the large airlines. He was deeply impressed by Dr. Frank
N. D. Buchman's Moral Rearmament movement. He based his
life on the four absolutes of that movement—Absolute Honesty, Absolute Purity, Absolute Unselfishness, and Absolute
Love.

His friends in the Movement told him: "Sit down each
morning for God's guidance." He was intensely interested. He
asked various members of the Movement how to achieve such
guidance. They told him to sit down each morning and write
down his thoughts and his schedule for the day, checking each
item against the four absolutes. He tried it for several months,
but each morning he felt sure that what he got was simply
wishful thinking, out of his own conscious mind.

Then one morning he accidentally hit upon a technique
that relaxed his body deeply. Thereupon, he writes,

> I received God guidance. I had several questions
> that had been written down for some time and for
> which I was seeking the proper answer. I knew that
> morning that I had received guidance from a higher
> source. For the next year, it would often take ten or
> twenty minutes to get completely relaxed. That first
> day is the time I consider that I just stopped blunder-
> ing through life. This first accomplishment opened
> many doors for me. I started investigating things that
> previously I had completely refused to consider. . . .
> I feel that the truest thing in my life is my own guid-
> ance, when I am in deep relaxation. I sometimes hear
> the small, quiet voice; sometimes in picture form or
> in moving picture form, both black and white and in

color, visualized. Sometimes it is on a scale with "yes" on one side and "no" on the other side of the scale. I consider that I get into three stages of depth in guidance. Most of the time my conscious brain makes small decisions. I consider the second depth or stage, that of my sub-conscious or the soul, as making the decision. . . . The third stage I compare with the spirit or some super-conscious intelligence. I seldom get in this deep.

Guidance prevented a disastrous accident

The following is an example of the crucially significant guidance that Mr. Wipprecht has been receiving since he learned to apply the technique of listening prayer:

About June 2, 1952, in the morning in a motel at Gatlinburg, I wrote in my guidance book, "Remain sensitive throughout the day and you will be guided through a safe day." I read it to my family, and advised them that I would do all of the driving that day. We were on our way to Lafayette, Indiana. About 2:00 P.M. we were coming through the hills and had been following a large, fast moving van for several miles. The two-lane highway emerged on an approximate two-mile stretch of straight highway which had been built through the center of an oak forest. These trees, 16 to 24 inches in trunk diameter, had been left standing 10 to 12 feet on each side of the pavement. I started to pass and our bodies were just about even with the rear of this fast moving van when I received very strongly the thought, "Pull back." I stepped on the brake hard, and at the same time the truck swerved all the way to the left until one of the dual rear wheels hit dirt. It missed the nose of my Chrysler by less than one foot—twelve inches. I consider this the most important piece of guidance in my life. It saved three of us. Naturally, I very fervently said, "Thank you, Father."

This guided transaction was profitable

In general, spiritual guidance is not a useful aid in stock speculation. But those who are dedicated to the four absolutes, and who have learned to follow the Inner Light, find that their material needs are cared for. Mr. Wipprecht gives the following example:

> On July 27, 1953, I wrote in my guidance book, "Sell Commonwealth Edison." (I had 30 shares.) I was surprised and asked, "What shall I buy?" and got quiet. I wrote down "Lane Bryan." I did not know of such a stock, but later accepted it as Lane Bryant. On July 30th I sold the 30 shares of Commonwealth Edison that had been paying $30.00 a year dividend. I added a little over $500.00 on advice of the broker and bought 100 shares of Lane Bryant. That year I received $100.00 dividend, plus 5 more shares of the stock worth $15.25 per share, a total of $176.25. I still own the 105 shares of Lane Bryant. It is now priced at about $20.25 per share instead of $15.25 and is now paying $1.20 per year dividend, which amounts to a considerably improved investment by making the change.

He learned to seek guidance continually

Commenting on the above two examples, and on many other experiences that cannot be related here, Mr. Wipprecht observes:

> These things do not happen every day, and many days are routine. The first example that I mentioned above, taught me to try and stay open for guidance all the time. I try constantly to carry the thought, "I am always under direct inspiration. I make right decisions quickly." I try to keep this deeply imbued in my sub-conscious mind. It seems to work. . . .
> In the past two or three years I have adopted a

prayer that introduces me to complete relaxation immediately. I feel this prayer covers everything. It is:

"Eternal Father: Who committed to us the swift and solemn trust of life, may we recognize that the hour for serving Thee is always present. May we wake to the instant claims of Thy holy will, not waiting for tomorrow, but yielding today, immediately."

FAMILY FINANCES CALL FOR SPIRITUAL GUIDANCE

Do you ever yield to worry, fear, and discouragement about the problems of finding the right employment, winning promotion, meeting the family bills, and finding how and where to purchase what the family needs? Here are some typical experiences of ways in which the spiritually guided person can be freed from anxieties, and can find the right way to go forward successfully in what otherwise would often be a bewildering maze of difficulties and frustrations:

Prayer guided Mrs. Gunn to the job she wanted

Mrs. Florence Gunn, of Hume, Missouri, tells this experience:

> In 1945 I wanted to work for Unity School of Practical Christianity at Kansas City and moved there for that purpose, but there was no vacancy. Then, just as I was asking by spot prayer for guidance as to which of two other jobs to take, I suddenly snapped my fingers and said, "I'm going to Unity and will be at work there by three o'clock." When I got there, the girl at the desk said, "How did you know that there was a vacancy? We have only known it ourselves for ten minutes." I got the job and it was very helpful to me in many ways.

Prayer guided Mr. Norgaard to change his employment

To obtain guidance about when to quit may be as important as being led in finding new employment. Peter W. Norgaard, of Glenview, Illinois, tells this experience:

> In struggling to find the right work in 1955, and having already spent five months on various sales jobs with little or no income, I was for two months working for an employment office in Chicago. I had high hopes for placements and commissions, but I had realized only $90 during that time. With family finances in desperate shape, I prayed one evening that I would be given a very definite and final answer whether I should try to continue in this work. The following morning I had scarcely entered the office when my employer confronted me as to the wisdom of my continuing on and suggested that I would do better for myself in some other pursuit. It was an hour or more later, while finalizing my work, that I recalled my spiritual request of the evening before, and was almost stunned at the speed, definiteness and exactness with which this prayer had been answered. In my own feeling, and from previous prayer-answer experiences, I am convinced that this was in no way circumstantial.

Mrs. Norgaard has been a close partner with her husband in the use of prayer for guidance and help.

Prayer brought help in a family-finance crisis

Most families, especially when the children are young and the wage-earner is still climbing up the lower rungs of the promotion ladder, run into money shortages. Sometimes hoped-for income fails to materialize. Sometimes unlooked for needs demand funds. People who have learned the power of guidance and help come to a deep assurance, based on repeated experience, that urgent needs will be met if spiritual help is sought. Mrs. Norgaard gives an example:

In the summer of 1955, at the time of a complete professional reorientation and several months without any income, we prayed and meditated that another personal loan would not be necessary but that somehow our needs would be met for another month. Within three hours, the mail brought us our income tax refund that we had not expected until later.

Prayer brought crucial help in the purchase of a truck

Those who live by guidance find often that the plan into which they have been led develops difficulties. That is a sign to seek further guidance. Mrs. Norgaard tells about such an experience in their guided working out of their income problem:

> The same summer, in July 1955, we started a new service business that required the purchase of a used truck. We stated our need specifically in our prayers and meditation as to the amount we could spend on it, the size and type of truck, the time deadline we had to have it; in other words, turned the locating of the truck over to a higher power. By becoming extremely alert to intuition, my eyes fell on a newspaper ad while waiting on the phone one day. Among over 20 passenger cars, this dealer advertised a used truck of the type we had in mind as well as the price. He never deals in these trucks nor would we ever have looked up his place otherwise. When I checked the date of the ad, it was three weeks old. We obtained the truck at an even reduced price and had it in running shape a few days before our set deadline.

Hunches guided Mrs. Norgaard to needed bargains
for her family

When income is meager and needs are great, the mother, as family purchasing agent, needs great guidance in finding the largest values for the smallest expenditures. Mrs. Norgaard

gives the following summary of her experiences in finding
solutions for such problems:

> Whenever we need articles for our home or cloth-
> ing for the family, I see it clearly in my mind, as to
> type, color, size, etc. Then I get hunches out of the
> "blue sky" as to where to go and find the exact article
> as I had seen it in my mind, in places like thrift shops
> and church rummage sales. To mention a particular
> instance, not unusual but the latest in a continuous
> series:
>
> July 8, 1957 my intuition told me to visit a par-
> ticular thrift shop where I had previously found
> many articles. My conscious mind, however, at first
> said no, as I did not have any specific need in mind.
> Something though made me go there, only to find out
> that the thrift shop building has been sold and that
> the entire stock was on sale for two more days only.
> Not exactly knowing what to look for, I happened to
> ask one of the ladies for winter coats. She brought me
> several used ones in fine condition. Suddenly I re-
> alized that I would need a new winter coat come fall,
> so here I purchased a beautiful all-alpaca lined cash-
> mere coat for five dollars, another cashmere coat for
> one dollar, plus several pieces of clothing for my hus-
> band and children.

SPIRITUAL POWER CAN DIRECT
PHYSICAL FORCES

The above principle now rests upon validated evidence obtained in parapsychological laboratories. Perhaps it may seem
incongruous to have that demonstration depend upon such
trivial acts as dice-throwing. But the evidence thus obtained
is incontrovertible. The phenomenon is called "psychokinesis."

If the human will can bring it about that a chosen series of
faces appears on freely thrown dice more often than can be
explained, by any reasonable supposition, as due to chance,
what are the limits to the possible effects that superhuman
purpose may have upon physical events?

An Old Testament story is illuminated by parapsychology

In the book of Judges (Chapters 6 to 8) there is an account of a time when the Midianites, enemies of Israel, were destroying their crops and plundering their livestock, so that the children of Israel were being impoverished. Then the Spirit of Jehovah came upon Gideon and said: "Go and save Israel from the hand of Midian: have I not sent thee?" But Gideon wanted parapsychological evidence that he had in truth been chosen. The biblical account of the experiment that he proposed and carried out is as follows:

> And Gideon said unto God, If thou wilt save Israel by my hand, as thou hast spoken, behold I will put a fleece of wool on the threshing-floor; if there be dew on the fleece only, and it be dry upon all the ground, then shall I know that thou wilt save Israel by my hand, as thou hast spoken.
>
> And it was so; for he rose up early on the morrow, and pressed the fleece together, and wrung the dew out of the fleece, a bowlful of water.

But Gideon wanted a control experiment to check his first results:

> And Gideon said unto God, Let not thine anger be kindled against me, and I will speak but this once: let me make trial, I pray thee, but this once with the fleece; let it now be dry only upon the fleece, and upon all the ground let there be dew. And God did so that night: for it was dry upon the fleece only, and there was dew on all the ground.

Prayer brought protection from a devastating storm

The dew-line around Gideon's fleece finds a remarkable parallel in the experience that Mrs. Dorothy D. Shaw, of Garrettsville, Ohio, tells:

A wild, tornado-like storm suddenly struck our little town about five o'clock in the afternoon of August 18, 1956. Many trees were knocked down, roofs ripped loose, and buildings damaged. Telephone lines were down, electric power was off for twenty-four hours, and county aid was brought in to work for several days clearing the streets for traffic.

The fine old trees on the acre of ground surrounding our 95-year-old house are precious to us. I stood at the kitchen door that afternoon, wondering at the sudden dark and yellowing sky, and nervous about the lightning. There was an electric excitement in the air. We were all at home, son and daughter on vacation from their colleges, my husband and I. I was praying silently (and fervently) for protection.

With a roar the storm hit . . . looking down across the lawn I saw the fine old towering elm tree on my neighbor's lawn split down the middle. It was a dreadful sight. But fascinating. My prayer gained intensity as I stared at the wild scene.

Distinctly, the inner voice said: "Do not look at the evil." I knew it for clear, definite direction in a time of great need, and I turned away from the door. It took a wrenching effort to do this—the drama of the storm was so tremendous. Later, our daughter said that she could not imagine resisting the impulse to watch the show.

I went to a secluded part of the house and stilled my mind and accepted the simple prayer given me by the inner voice: "The Hand of Peace is over all." I remained in this single prayer, in the quiet (using my will to shut out the crashing and shrieking sounds of the storm), until it was all over. It was not a long time, but it seemed interminable. Several weeks later, I learned that my husband was withdrawn, in another room, in prayer for protection.

Each of us was visualizing, as we stayed deep in prayer. I "saw" steadily, clearly, the great Divine Hand covering the home place, and it was effortless.

A quarter of an hour later, when we went out and viewed the damage in the neighborhood, I realized (with deep regret) that my prayer had been too limited. All around us were fallen trees. Only a few twigs and small branches had come down on our property. We had even benefited . . . the big old three-story barn had the roof pulled slightly out of line, and the insurance settlement took care of this and paid two-thirds of the cost of a long-needed new roof.

The most important result of this experience in spiritual guidance was to establish clearly in my mind the command *not* to study evil—that is, not to "face up" to evil, not to "battle the adversary."

A DIFFICULT PERSONAL RELATIONSHIP WAS RESOLVED BY PRAYER

Sometimes the disciplining of human emotions and of social relationships presents problems even more difficult than those engendered by the weather. An example is presented by a high school teacher, in an experience that she relates as follows:

In September 1951 I was transferred to a high school where I was to serve as the treasurer and handle all affairs of money. A certain teacher had been handling school accounts, but the authorities felt that he had better stay in the classroom where he taught book-keeping—and not work on the school ledger, etc. The principal asked him to show me how the books were set up, how money was received and spent, and get me started. He was most cooperative and even drove me home after school. He was running an insurance business on the side that he said netted him more annually than his salary as a teacher. Two evenings later he rang my door-bell and came in with a bulging brief-case and asked me if I would be so kind as to type up some bills and envelopes for his insurance work. He had brought along two big corned-beef sandwiches that he revealed after several hours of intense work had transpired, and then asked me if I would be so kind as to make some coffee. He said his secretary was ill and he didn't know how he would have managed these monthly statements and bills if I hadn't helped him out.

I soon found out from others that he never hired a secretary but spent his leisure hours hunting up volunteer help. I decided that I wasn't a volunteer of this activity and took it up with what I call my Spirit Guides, in prayer. I repeated my petition for about two weeks, asking release from the association of that person, without any harm coming to him.

I met him each morning with a smile and never indicated that I was asking for deliverance from him and his endless requests and excuses to come to my apartment.

I began to feel comfortable about the matter and felt that it need not be continued. On a Monday morning two weeks later he received a transfer to a school that has extended days (a Vocational school) and extra pay. His application had been on file for over a year and action had just been taken. He considered it rather sudden. I knew that action had been directed.

PRAYER GUIDED HER TO JUSTICE
FOR HER CLIENT

Most of the examples given thus far in this chapter have related to personal and family problems. Fully as important, however, is the bearing of spiritual guidance on the solution of social problems and on success in social service. An example in this area is the following:

Olive H. Rabe, of Boulder, Colorado, writes that the clearest case of spiritual guidance in her experience happened toward the end of 1919. She describes it as follows:

I had been working as a lawyer on the staff of the Legal Aid Society of Chicago, and when I opened my own office I took one of the cases with me to handle. So much work was involved that I knew none of the overworked lawyers at the Legal Aid could manage to put enough time on it to prepare it thoroughly. The client had lost the use of his right arm through an industrial accident and had received an award from the Workmen's Compensation Bureau. The point was to collect the award. The employer had not carried any compensation insurance, and shortly after the accident he had filed a petition in bankruptcy, telling the injured employee that he would have to file a claim in bankruptcy and take his chances along with the other unsecured creditors. As there was a mortgage and several other liens entitled to payment ahead of the ordinary creditors, it was evident that they would collect nothing. Unless I could establish that my client had a preferred claim, his case was hopeless.

After briefing all the federal cases on the point, I talked them over with a lawyer experienced in bankruptcy cases. He told me I was wasting my time trying to make out a case for priority of payment because it was clear that the law was against it. Still I felt there must be some way to get justice for a man who had suffered a permanent loss in earning capacity. I went back to the quiet of the Law Library and started to write a trial brief without a solitary decision in my favor. But it was no use. I had to admit that legally the claim of priority was hopeless. I sat there staring at my papers and realizing that I could do nothing. Then, although I prayed but seldom in those years, I turned to God in desperation and asked Him to show me the way out. The answer came so clearly that there was no doubt about it, and I quickly jotted down the line of argument that would by-pass the unfavorable decisions.

The petition I filed claiming priority was hotly contested, but Judge Kenesaw M. Landis was impressed by the justice of the claim and ordered it to be paid in full.

COULD STILL MORE ADEQUATE GUIDANCE
BE ACHIEVED?

An important question may, perhaps, have come into your mind as you have been reading the experiences given in this chapter. How did these people get into some of these difficulties if they were using spiritual guidance? The answer seems fairly obvious: These people, like many of the rest of us, need to learn to use guidance more consistently, more receptively, and more effectively. Now that we have increasing evidence that spiritual guidance can be real, and now that we are in a position to see, more and more clearly, how it has worked in the lives of others, the opportunity is given us to test out better and better methods, and to become more and more fully aligned with the Divine Purpose, in which our own lives can find true and glorious fulfillment.

IT IS YOUR PRIVILEGE TO PROVIDE
YOUR OWN PROOF

The case stories that you have been reading in this chapter give evidence that is sincere and honest. But it is not evidence that would be accepted as conclusive in a law court or in a scientific investigation. All we have here is testimony as to human experiences, interpreted by people who had faith, and who found themselves encouraged, inspired, guided, and saved.

The very heart of the spiritual adventure is linked up with the fact that if you too would have such guidance and such blessing, you must seek it for yourself. We have been told that those who seek find. That is an hypothesis to be tested. The rest of the chapters in this book tell how to test it.

Chapter 6

Listening Prayer Can Give

You God's Guidance

Speak to Him, thou, for He hears,
And Spirit with Spirit can meet;
Closer is He than breathing,
And nearer than hands or feet.*

WE ARE IN THE MIDST OF EVERLASTING LIFE

In the chapters that you have been reading, we have been exploring together some of the basic facts and beliefs on which our spiritual adventure must be based. Two crucial conclusions place our lives in a spiritual perspective.

First, we have found ourselves confronting the conclusion that we live and move and have our being within the consciousness of God. Our ultimate destiny in the amazing adventure in which we find ourselves must depend upon our learning to come into effective communion and working relations with the Creator, of Whose consciousness our lives are a part.

---

* Alfred, Lord Tennyson, *The Higher Pantheism.*

A second discovery brings home even more fully the realization that we must learn to live the spiritual life. We have found that it is wholly reasonable to believe that human personalities survive bodily death, and that they go on in a progressive spiritual adventure. Our present earthly life is found to be a vestibule—a training school in which we have the opportunity, while living here in our physical bodies, to learn at least the beginnings of the two great skills of living: first, how to live lovingly; and, second, how to live spiritually.

If these are true facts about the life-challenge that confronts us, then we, like the Great Teacher, must "be about Our Father's business." And if we are to do His will, what we need, first and most to learn, is how to be guided by His Spirit.

THE MEANING OF LISTENING PRAYER

Right now, no matter what the problems of your life may be, there is a power that can carry you forward with courage and with joy. But you have to learn to make contact with that power. Sometimes people have had to come to the very threshold of despair in order to find it. At that theshold they have cried out: "Oh, God help me!" And out of despair has come the wonder, the joy and the power of God's love.

Prayer is more than a sincere desire. It is laying hold upon super-human power. It is the actual making of contact with life-changing and wonder-working power. This is what we seek. This is what is available to us if we lay hold upon the promised help which so many, down through the ages, have found.

THIS GIRL SAVED HER LIFE-HAPPINESS
BY LISTENING PRAYER

Myrtle was a junior in college. She was deeply in love with a boy who was a sophomore. She was earning grades that were above average in her courses, while he was just barely getting enough C's to stay in college. But they were very deeply in love, and they planned to get married as soon as he graduated.

This was just before World War II, while American munitions factories were working day and night to supply Great Britain with the ammunition to hold Hitler and Nazism back from invading England. The boy's parents said to each other: "Why should we pay out tuition to keep our boy struggling along on a barely passing average in college when workers are desperately needed to save Western civilization?" They answered their own question by telling the boy that he would have to take a job in a munitions factory in Pittsburgh, and thus do his part to make the world safe for democracy.

He took the move philosophically, but the girl felt deeply injured. She said to herself, indignantly: "His mother and father are just trying to break up our engagement! This is just an excuse to put 400 miles between him and me, so that they can marry him off to some other girl! I'm not going to stand for it!"

So she sat down and wrote some very bitter letters to her boy friend and to his parents. And, of course, that made her feel more dejected, more miserable, and more defeated.

It happened that she was taking a course in Religion, in which the professor believed that the students ought actually to practice prayer. In one of his lectures he gave them advice like the following:

> Do you believe that there is a Power above all human power, a loving intelligence which responds to human needs, when open-hearted and open-minded seekers reach out toward Him?
>
> Well, the belief that there is such a Power is an hypothesis that can be tested by experiment. I want you to test it. Each one of you has problems to face. I want you to pick out the one that seems to you to be most difficult and most important. I want you to try an experiment in seeking superhuman help and guidance on that problem.
>
> On each of the next ten days, I want you to take fifteen minutes and go apart into a quiet place where you will not be interrupted. In this quiet place, I

want you to relax very deeply. When you get relaxed, I want you to reach out to this Superhuman Power, and ask Him what you ought to do about this most important problem which you are facing.

Keep a record each day of just what you do to get relaxed, just how you put the question to the Higher Power whose reality you are testing—and just what results (if any) you receive.

The girl said to herself: "Well, I sure enough have a problem! I'll see whether I can get any guidance about how to save my engagement from going to smash!"

So she carried out the professor's instructions for 15 minutes every day. She did it for nine days, and she drew nine blanks. No illumination came. She felt as baffled and perplexed as ever.

When the tenth day came she said to herself: "Well, the prof said to do it ten times. It hasn't done any good the first nine times—but I'm desperate. Here I stand on the brink of despair. This once more I'm going to let go and ask God."

So she sat in the big upholstered chair in her study, when nobody else was around. She relaxed as deeply as she could. She made her mind open and asked once more: "What is the matter? What ought I to do?"

Then suddenly the answer came. Later on she wrote an unsolicited letter to her professor, telling of her experience:

> As I sat there in despair, and yet reaching out blindly for help, I suddenly felt as though a flash of lightning had illuminated my life and my problem. Suddenly these words sprang into my mind: "I'm the one who is to blame!"
>
> I got up, went to my desk, and wrote a letter to my boy friend's mother. I told her how ashamed of myself I was. I told her that I knew I had been mean and suspicious and antagonistic, and I wanted her to forgive me.
>
> By return mail I got a letter from her. She wrote that she had always wanted to have a daughter, and

that she had hoped that I would be that daughter.

Within two weeks we had arranged to have her and my mother both come to the campus and get acquainted with each other. My fiancé wrote to me one of the happiest letters I had ever had from him. Well, the outcome of the whole thing was that we got married a year earlier than I had ever hoped might be possible!

THE PATH OUT OF THE THICKET WAS BRIGHTLY LIGHTED

Every such answer to listening prayer is unique. No two cases are exactly alike. Your problem is certain to be different in various ways from the problem that anyone else brings to the Mercy Seat. But the wonderful thing about listening prayer is that if you can learn to give yourself to it wholly and unreservedly, the answer to *your* need can come flashing into your mind—along with the courage and the power to carry out the indicated solution.

Here is one more actual case to illustrate how this Power and this Wisdom can come to the listening heart and mind.

A young engineer (whom we will call Ben) was having trouble with his studies. He had plenty of intelligence to master his assignments, his grades in high school and in the first year of college had shown that. But he had acquired a roommate who was far more interested in playing poker than he was in getting an engineering degree. Ben didn't want to be a prude, and he didn't want to be a wet blanket. So he allowed himself to get into a series of poker games in which he wasted a lot of study time, and also a good deal of his quite scarce allowance money. As a result, he flunked a quiz, and the professor gave him a rather serious warning.

Ben had been brought up by an idealistic, religious mother. She had died when he was in his early teens, but the memory of her faith and of her courageous life still had powerful linkages with the deeper layers of his personality.

After he got back the quiz paper with its failing grade, Ben went out for a walk in the woods. The path passed near a thicket of brambles on the edge of a swamp. He looked over, and thought to himself: "In my struggle to become an engineer, I feel just as if I had been caught in a thicket of thorns like that one over there."

Then, suddenly, he remembered how his mother had taught him to pray. Impulsively he felt these words forming themselves in his mind: "Mother, what ought I to do to get out of this jam I've gotten myself into?"

Instantly, still in his inner mind, he thought that he was hearing his mother's voice, in her familiar tones, saying: "These words are part of the eternal truth: 'Out of each thicket leads a path; and to each summit a sharp and thorny way ascends.'"

To Ben, those words became a continuing message. To him they meant this: "No matter how perplexing and painful the difficulty may be, there is always a way out. But the true path will always be likely to lie through difficulties and dangers."

THE BEST APPROACH TO LISTENING PRAYER

You, also, who are reading these words, have problems on which you need help. Quite possibly you also find that the help you need is often greater than you can readily obtain from human sources. What is the best way for you to go about seeking an answer by means of listening prayer?

Preparation is the first step

If you engage in listening prayer, you do so always with a purpose. You have a question to which you need an answer. You have a problem for which you need a solution. You are seeking God's guidance and help.

Long ago, wise men found out that "Heaven helps those that help themselves." God gave us our brains, our eyes, and our intelligence. He gave us "spades" to dig with. Before seeking illumination in listening prayer, you, as a wise seeker, will carefully and industriously do your preliminary "spadework." To find true wisdom we need to learn to use a library, with all its marvelous modern aids for finding swiftly what has been discovered by those who have gone before us. We need to talk with wise friends who may have knowledge about the problem on which we are seeking guidance. We may quite likely find it helpful to go out and do some field work—visit places, examine objects, and question people who may have knowledge to give to us.

But let us suppose that you or I have done all that we humanly can to find the true answer to our problem. How then may we, with real effectiveness, start reaching out to Superhuman Wisdom?

Listening prayer may be thought of as tuning in on God. In some ways it is like tuning in upon very faint radio signals. You have to get rid of static and of ordinary noise if you want to get a clear message under such conditions. It is difficult to receive radio waves successfully if a thunderstorm is creating static. Even the passing of airplanes can disturb TV reception. In much the same way, the person who seeks to receive the superhuman message, in listening prayer, must get rid of interference and of static. And among the worst kinds of interference with listening prayer are resentment, antagonism, and hatred. Therefore—

Reconciliation comes before meditation

The Great Teacher put it this way:

> If you remember, even when offering your gift at the altar, that your brother has any grievance against you, leave your gift at the very altar and go away; first be reconciled to your brother, and then come back and offer your gift.

Now why did the ancients offer gifts at altars? Anthropologists tell us that this is a very ancient custom, going back far beyond the dawn of history. To offer a gift at an altar was a symbolic act. To "offer a sacrifice" means, literally, to make a gift sacred. Sacred things are those which have in them the

power and presence of God. Offering a gift at the altar was
thus a ritual act whose purpose was to bring the worshipper
into living contact with God Himself.

But this living contact with God is exactly what we seek in
prayer. Quite usually people plunge into prayer without taking note of this vital instruction given by Jesus. Over toward
the end of the New Testament, John gives the reason why
reconciliation must come first:

> He who will not love his brother whom he has seen,
> cannot possibly love the God Whom he has never
> seen.

Jesus himself put it positively in his last conversation with
the Disciples, as reported in the Fourth Gospel:

> If you remain in me and my words remain in you,
> then ask whatever you like and you shall have it. . . .
> This is what I command you, to love one another.

It can be put quite simply. Prayer is an act in which we
seek to come into harmony with God—harmony of thought,
harmony of word, and harmony of action. To achieve this harmony is an outreaching act by the one who prays; it brings a
vital response from God Himself. But since God is Love,
neither you, nor I, nor anyone can expect to receive His power
and illumination unless we are deeply and thoroughly attuned
to love. If we hold hatred, resentment, and antagonism, that is
a barrier that shuts the door against the very thing we are
seeking. First, then, be reconciled; when that is achieved, we
are ready to go forward in prayer.

He went apart to pray

Quite often true prayer takes place in groups. Jesus himself
is reported to have prayed often in the presence of other people, and many examples could be quoted from the Old Testament, and from other religious annals. But we have seen that
tuning in on God is (in some ways) similar to what the operator of a radio reeiving set must do in tuning in on some

message from a remote sending station. The signals are extremely delicate and subtle. To receive the message clearly, the operator must get rid of interference and of static. The interruptions, the hubbub, the distractions and the interferences from the outer world, can drown out the message.

It was for this reason that Jesus himself, over and over again, "went apart into the mountains to pray." He told his listeners:

> When you pray, go into your room and shut the door. Pray to your Father, Who is in secret, and your Father Who sees what is secret will reward you.

Let flesh retire

The Quakers know a good deal about listening prayer. One famous Quaker was John Greenleaf Whittier. He wrote a hymn that has been familiar to millions, beginning with the lines:

> Dear Lord and Father of mankind, forgive our feverish ways. . . .

Later in that same hymn, Whittier tells us to relax if we would hear the Voice of God:

> Let sense be dumb; let flesh retire;
> Speak through the earthquake
> Wind and fire
> Oh, still, small voice of calm.

To "let flesh retire" means to relax—deeply, profoundly. The relaxing is for the purpose of quieting down all of the disturbances of mind and muscle that interfere with receiving "the still, small voice" in which intuition speaks.

Listening prayer, and the deep prayer about which we shall learn in later chapters, are far more powerful and rewarding than the forms of prayer that most people casually use. And one of the vital elements that make listening prayer and deep prayer so full of illumination and power is profound relaxation. Those who have begun to win the blessings of these forms of prayer find that the following acts are of fundamental help:

Let go, and let God. Cast all your care on Him; He cares for you. Think of yourself as a little child, enfolded in the arms of love, letting go of your body as a child, falling asleep in its mother's arms, becomes limp, and serene, and utterly peaceful. Remember the ancient words:

Peace I leave with you; my peace I give unto you.
Let not your heart be troubled, neither let it be afraid.

For several minutes, let that peace flow into your body and your mind. Keep on letting go. As your body becomes more and more inert, and relaxed, and limp, your mind can become more and more detached, and clear, and receptive. In quietness and confidence shall be your strength.

The deep-breath method

A relatively simple and highly effective method of relaxation has been developed by a professional colleague at Duke University. Having assumed the specified posture, in the dark, quiet room, free from interruption, Dr. Jensen's procedure is as follows:

Close the eyes. Breathe in very deeply and steadily. As you breathe in, think of *heaviness* and *peace* as streaming into your fingers, hands, and arms. You do not need to use these words, even silently to yourself. Merely concentrate your entire attention serenely on the feeling of heaviness and peace streaming from the tips of your fingers up into your arms. During the first taken-in breath, think of the heaviness and peace as streaming up as far as your elbows. Then let your breath out.

Breathe in a second time in the same way, this time thinking of the heaviness and peace as streaming up your arms from your fingertips to your shoulders. During the third breath, think of the heaviness and peace as penetrating into your chest from both shoulders and meeting at the centre. During the fourth in-breathing think of it as spreading down through your body to your solar plexus. During the next in-breathing think of the heaviness and peace as streaming down from the solar plexus through your legs, to your toes. During the next in-breathing, think of the heaviness as spreading upward from your chest through your head.

After these six breathings, taken in this way, your whole body should be profoundly relaxed, and you should be ready for the next step in whatever exercise you are carrying on.

THE CENTRAL STEPS IN LISTENING PRAYER

Invocation comes first in the act of prayer itself

Every true prayer begins by reaching out to God. When Jesus taught his disciples the prayer that has become the most widely used in the Western World, he began with the words: "Our Father, Who art in heaven."

This outreach toward the Source from which we seek help must not be a mere empty rattling off of words. The words are helpful if they are true vehicles of the spirit. What matters is the outreach of the heart and mind and strength, asking and listening.

Ask and ye shall receive; seek and ye shall find; knock and it shall be opened unto you.

Dedication carries us beyond reconciliation

We have seen that reconciliation is essential before we can even begin to practice listening prayer truly. The purpose is to remove the resentments, the antagonisms, the acts and attitudes of anger, exploitation, and injustice that have set up barriers between us and God. Reconciliation is like eliminating static in a radio receiving set. It is negative in the sense that it means getting rid of something false and destructive.

But tuning in on God is basically positive. Just as your radio set can be adjusted to the wave-length of the incoming message, so the act of tuning in on God depends upon bringing ourselves into harmony with the purposes of God. That is what is meant by *dedication*.

Christians generally have found spiritual help in thinking of the death of Jesus on the Cross as having been an *atonement* for the sins of mankind. That great word takes on clearer meaning when we break it up into its vital parts: *at-one-ment*. The vital need of the spiritual seeker is to come to be at one with God. A hymn that has been a favorite from of old carries the refrain: "O be ye reconciled to God." Ralph Waldo Trine wrote a book, named *In Tune with the Infinite,* that has been of help to vast numbers of people.

Our petitions—our prayers asking for help—have been prone to take the form of begging God to come over and side with us, to give us help in carrying out our often self-centered and shortsighted purposes. But the very keynote of true prayer is that the worshipper shall tune in on God's purposes. If you and I come into harmony with the will of God, if we make ourselves instruments of His purpose, then we may become channels of His power.

Center your consciousness utterly on God

Relaxation, invocation, and dedication (if truly performed) have brought you into the presence of God, in a spirit that seeks humbly to do His will. In this state you are ready to seek and receive God's guidance. You are ready to "lay your burden on the Lord." You are bringing your problem to the Mercy Seat.

But listening prayer can be effective only for those who truly listen. This means that all wandering thoughts, all ideas and feelings not directly and vitally connected with our problem, shall be excluded from our minds. Concentration is not a matter of knitting one's brow and setting one's jaw. Such actions would violate the basic condition of relaxation. Concentration simply means the exclusion of all thought-wandering, the shutting out of everything irrelevant to the problem on which you are consulting God.

Meditation is the very heart of listening prayer

All of the preceding steps have been by way of leading up to this crucial point at which, in your state of deep relaxation and concentration, after the acts of invocation and dedication, you place your problem before God.

Whereas concentration consists in exclusion of the irrelevant, meditation consists in holding the attention steadily upon the relevant, lighted by the Inner Light. It consists in centering your thoughts upon the problem in hand and then listening receptively for guidance—watching for illumination.

Perhaps the simplest way to think of meditation is to put it into the form of asking the question which states your problem, and then listening for the answer. Meditation is a serene, poised, receptive state of mind. The answer comes out of the Silence.

FOLLOWING UP YOUR MEDITATION

Illumination is the harvest and the reward

After you have succeeded in becoming calm, deep down inside, and after you have centered your attention serenely upon the stated question, in the Divine Presence, the flash of illumination may be expected.

A beginner quite often misses it because he does not realize that it has come. One of the main difficulties in listening prayer is that quite often people fail to recognize the flash. Very few (and these only rarely) attain from meditation any blinding vision, any "angel visitant," any rapturous sense of sudden and complete knowledge. Usually, the one who is praying hears no celestial trumpet; he sees no fiery letters written in the sky. He just gets a bright idea. But that bright idea *is* the answer; it *is* the flash of illumination.

What does happen, to most of us most of the time, is a clearing of inner insight. Obstacles begin to melt away. In the serenely quiet inner consciousness, fresh and living ideas begin to spring up. Quite often the needed flash comes after you have stopped trying to get it, when you have started thinking about something else. Sometimes the new insight will spring into your mind when you are waking up from sleep in the morning. (A very good idea, by the way, is to keep a pencil and a pad of paper near the head of your bed, so that when these ideas do spring up during your awakening, you may note them down before they evaporate.)

Quite often, one of the major results of listening prayer is a surge of courage and energy that empowers the seeker to come to grips with his problem, and to deal with it creatively, sensing the presence and the guidance of God. Often you may find that listening prayer leads simply to a deep, peaceful sense that everything is going to be all right, that what you need to do is to go ahead and follow the Light as it comes, without worrying about the outcome. Do your best, and trust God. If that peaceful assurance comes to you, accept it gratefully as His answer to your listening prayer.

Contemplation follows illumination

In the Gospel according to Matthew, an account is given of how Jesus took Peter, James, and John into a high mountain apart, and was there transfigured before them. As the vision drew to a close, Peter said to Jesus: "Lord, it is good for us to be here. . . ."

When listening prayer has reached its summit in illumination, bringing either new insight, a new surge of courage and energy, a new feeling of deep peace and security, or perhaps all three of these, it is good to hold the mind steady for a while in the Divine Presence. This period of contemplation can serve several purposes. First, it can deepen the memory of the experience, allowing the illumination to sink deep into consciousness, so that it will become a source of strength for future needs. Second, it can help to fix in the mind of the seeker the insight which otherwise may swiftly evaporate, as dreams so often do just after one has remembered them on

awaking in the morning. Illumination has an ineffable quality. It is prone to vanish unless the seeker brings it down into
the embodiment of words and plans. Third, contemplation
can bring about a creative organization of the illumination
into a purpose and a plan, by means of which it can later be
put into action.

One other value in contemplation is that it provides an opportunity to give thanks to the Father Spirit from Whom help
has come. The sense of communion can be vivid and warm,
immediately after the one who prays has become aware of the
living and helping contact.

Verification is a vital step

Not every intuition can be trusted. For example, innumerable inventors have believed that they have received flashes
of intuition telling them how to create perpetual-motion ma-
chines. But no honest and successful working model for such
a machine has ever been offered to the United States Patent
Office. Among religious intuitions that prophets have regarded
as genuine, Mohammed apparently believed sincerely that he
received inspirations from Allah through the Angel Gabriel.
Yet his revelations about propagating the Islamic faith by warfare seem diametrically opposite to Christian revelations about
non-violence.

Quite often, people who believe themselves to be acting
under divine guidance are merely giving vent to their own
unconscious self-seeking and self-aggrandizing purposes. Because such things do occur so often, it is vital that the sincere
thinker shall find ways to verify his illumination, to make as
sure as possible that it is genuine and wholesome, not distorted
and destructive.

In the early Christian churches many self-announced prophets were proclaiming illuminations that they insisted they had
received from God, but which often were of doubtful value.
The Apostle Paul gave a basic piece of advice about this problem when he wrote to the Thessalonians:

Never disdain prophetic revelations, but test them
all, retaining what is good and abstaining from whatever kind is evil.

But how can the illuminations received in listening prayer
be subjected to any trustworthy test? Several useful steps can
be listed to that end:

(a) If, during your period of contemplation or later, you
feel any doubt, or any vague uneasiness about your illumination, go back into the process of prayer; state your question
once more, and in deep relaxation and meditation listen once
more for the answer. Be ready with open mind to receive some
different guidance. If the same illumination as before returns,
perhaps even stronger, then you need to take further steps.

(b) Talk your illumination over with some trusted friend
who also makes use of listening prayer, and is sensitive to divine guidance. Such a counsellor may not himself be able to
give you a clear-cut decision—and in any case, he should not
substitute his authority for the authority of your own Inner
Light. But communing with a fellow seeker is likely to clarify
the situation. And your sensitive friend may himself add illumination from his own sources which, you may realize, strength-
ens and corrects what has previously come to you.

(c) If your illumination seems to be validated by methods
(a) and (b), see whether you can try out the proposed action
on a small scale. Can you make some experiment which will
not be too costly, and yet which will help you to determine
whether the illumination you have received is right and good?

(d) If the illumination that has come to you through listening prayer remains strong, true and powerful under all
these tests, then you are called upon to put it into action.

Application is a consummation

One of the most ardent persecutors of the early Christians
was a young Pharisee named Saul of Tarsus. He was on his
way to Damascus to shut more Christians up in prison, and, if
possible, to condemn them to death. But in the midst of his

journey he had a vision of Jesus, who summoned him to be his minister and his emissary to the Gentiles.

The whole future of civilization hung upon Saul's decision as to what he would do about this illumination. If he had rejected the vision, and gone on persecuting the infant church, it seems highly probable that Christianity would never have spread into Europe. But, in telling King Agrippa about this experience, Saul (who thereafter was called Paul, the Apostle) said: "I was not disobedient unto the heavenly vision." He went out and planted Christianity in cities of Greece and at last in Rome. From Rome, Christianity became the decisive force from which sprang Western civilization.

We may put Paul's words into the imperative mood, and apply them to ourselves:

Be not disobedient to the heavenly vision!

Our own illuminations will doubtless be far less spectacular than that of Paul. But however humble we may be, the reward of following the Inner Light is that more light comes, whereas the punishment for quenching illumination is that the source of guidance more and more fades out within us.

THIS SUMS IT UP

In brief form, then, 12 steps of listening prayer may be summarized as follows:

Four steps are preliminary

1. Preparation comes first.
2. Reconciliation comes before meditation.
3. Isolation is important.
4. Relaxation is of crucial importance.

Four steps are central in listening prayer

5. Invocation comes first in the act of prayer itself.
6. Dedication is the second step.

7. Concentration is the shutting out of everything except your prayer problem.
8. Meditation is the very heart of listening prayer.

Your meditation needs fulfillment in four final steps

9. Illumination is the harvest and the reward.
10. Contemplation should follow illumination.
11. Verification is a vital step, after illumination and contemplation.
12. Application is a consummation.

Chapter 7

Prayer Can Bring

You Courage and Joy

The goal of true religion is the abundant life for all. That your joy can be full to overflowing if you follow the true path has been shown in Chapter 2. You must lose yourself in something greater than yourself. You must dedicate your life wholeheartedly to one or two or three great projects, recognizing that fulfillment of life comes through devotion to undertakings that involve hardship and danger as well as joyous achievement. Your main project may be your work, your marriage, parenthood, or public service. But if you are to enter fully into the life abundant, you must above all be dedicated to the spiritual quest.

WHY DO FAILURES OCCUR?

It is one thing to accept those ideals in theory. It is another thing to make them real in daily life.

Over and over again, in the Old Testament, we are told: "Be strong and of good courage." Almost all of us are courageous part of the time. It is easy to be cheerful when every-

83

thing is going well. Most of us even try to be brave when things begin to go amiss. Ella Wheeler Wilcox, a famous poet, has said:

> The man worthwhile
> Is the man who can smile
> When everything goes dead wrong.[1]

Over and over again, however, most of us fall down on the job of being courageous. It is safe to say that more than half of us get deeply discouraged and depressed at least once or twice a week.

Our misuse of emotional energy

The basic reason why we fail is really fairly simple. The energy of the universe is flowing through our bodies and our minds. When we take up our life activities we keep running into the difficulties and the hardships that are so vital a part of any good project. Hardships, dangers, failures, and disappointments rouse up energy in our bodies and minds. When we are thus roused, part of the divine vitality is coursing through our veins. Cosmic energy is ready to flow out at our finger tips. As sons and daughters of God we have the choice as to whether we will use this energy creatively, or let it go to waste, or let it flow into destructive actions.

People who get discouraged and depressed say to themselves, or to others, such things as these:

"It burns me up!"
"I'm hurt!"
"I'm disgusted!"
"I'm scared!"
"I'm worried!"
"I'm disheartened!"

Each one of these exclamations is an expression of a wrong attitude. Each one of them means that the one who says it has

---

[1] Permission granted by Rand McNally & Company, Conkey Division.

let the energy flow out in discouragement, in fear, in hatred, in worry, in damage to self or to others. To do these things is to get out of step with the Creative Spirit. Our joy is extinguished (at least for the time being) because we have not learned to take full control over our own conscious and unconscious attitudes, in the spirit, by the power, and under the guidance of Creative Love. The remedy for our failures is to be found in deep prayer.

SEARCHING FOR COURAGE BY COMMON SENSE

Discouragement comes from misuse of emotional energy. This can be corrected. Here are three steps by which, even without any conscious use of prayer, much can be achieved in the search for courage:

1. *Take an inventory* of the situation in which you find yourself. What is the real nature of the menace? How great is it? At what points is it open to solution? You also need to take an inventory of *yourself* as related to this menace. What are your strong points and your weaknesses in confronting this danger? How have you dealt with such menaces in the past? And what resources outside yourself might be made of use in coming to grips with the threatened danger?

2. *Let the possible lines of action which you might take become clear* in your own mind. Sometimes, in despair, one feels that he has been driven into a cul-de-sac—a blind alley from which no escape is possible. But this is always a delusion. No matter how bad a situation may seem, there are always several different possible ways of dealing with it. Out of your thoughtful inventory there should emerge a road map, an action diagram on which you see the paths that fork away from the danger spot on which you stand. Some of these paths will lead toward the light, some toward a deeper abyss; some toward primrose paths, some toward upward climbs. Whatever the paths are, in this second stage of changing menace to promise by courage, you need to see them as clearly as you can.

3. *Take the best road.* With the best insight you can summon, pick out from among the possible roads the one that seems most clearly to lead in the direction in which you really want to go. Having selected this road, throw all your energy into the endeavor to climb that hill, to progress along that line of action. If, by chance, you later find that you have chosen the wrong path, you can courageously choose again, knowing that, sooner or later, courage can produce a creative solution.

What can deep prayer add?

Much can be achieved by merely taking the three steps outlined above. But deep prayer taps in on resources much more powerful than merely one's own unconscious mind. Here are some of the ways in which prayer improves on the merely psychological approach.

First, that prase, "resources outside yourself," takes on new meaning. You have resolved to try the great experiment of taking God into your adventure. You are acting on the belief that His is a wisdom above all human wisdom, and that His is a power above all human power. Deep prayer is an act that reaches out to lay hold upon that wisdom and that power.

In the second step, deep prayer makes use of listening prayer for the purpose of "determining clearly in your own mind the possible lines of action you might take." With your courage you now combine faith. You act on the belief—and increasingly upon the experienced assurance—that out of any dark and threatening place there is a path into creative achievement. Then, in the very midst of deep prayer, you stop and listen to the voice of God; you watch for His light shining on your path, to show you which is the wise, loving, and creative way to take.

The third step is to "throw all your energy into the endeavor to progress along that best line of action." Here we come to the point where deep prayer heightens the power. To understand how we, each one of us, may lay hold upon that heightened power, we need to go into more detail about what are the steps in deep prayer, and how we may take them.

DEEP PRAYER, AND THE WINNING OF COURAGE

"A very present help in time of trouble"

"If God be with us, who can be against us?" is a thought that has given comfort to ancient seers and to modern seekers.

But it is a mistake to keep beseeching God to come over and join our side. The simple, wise, and honest thing to do is for us to go over and join up with God's side. If we do that, we and He stand together. Someone has said: "One, with God, is a majority." In the long run, out of the struggle, God's power, wisdom and love must be triumphant. Therefore, to align ourselves with the Divine Purpose brings it about that we cast off all ultimate reasons for discouragement.

The preliminary preparation

We have already considered, in Chapter 6, the steps by which we may come into touch with God in order to receive His guidance. Listening prayer and deep prayer both depend upon achieving working relations with Divine Wisdom and Power. The steps for removing our human barriers, and for opening up the channels of communication, are basic for any sort of real prayer. Reconciliation, isolation, invocation, and dedication, if carried out truly, prepare our hearts and minds to be filled with the courage and power of God.

Bodily relaxation is vitally important

In deep prayer, just as in listening prayer, it is vital that our physical bodies get out of our way. "Let flesh retire" is just as essential when we are seeking spiritual empowering of our courage as when we are seeking light on our path. How to breathe in serenity and peace has already been explained, in the chapter on listening prayer. Here is another simple method, in which you can achieve the needed relaxation by centering your thoughts for a few moments on four words. The four words are *relax, heavy, peace,* and *deeper.* You need to drink in the full meaning of each of these four words. You need to let that full meaning take possession of your mind and of your whole body.

Now take the four words, one at a time. The first is *RELAX!* As you say this word to yourself, watch for any tension anywhere in your fingers, hands, wrists, forehead, eyes, cheeks, mouth, or neck. If you find any tenseness anywhere in your body, just quietly let go of it. RELAX. Then bring to mind the deepest feelings of relaxation that you have previously experienced. Think about quietness, serenity, letting go. Let your whole body sink into deep restfulness. RELAX!

Now think about the second word—*HEAVY!* When you say this word silently to yourself, turn your attention to the feeling of bodily HEAVINESS which comes as relaxation is achieved. Say to yourself: "Your arms and legs are getting HEAVY like wooden beams . . . HEAVY like stone . . . HEAVY like lead." But remember that your spirit feels more and more released and free.

The third word is *PEACE!* As you keep on letting go of your muscles, a deep tide of PEACE flows into your body. As your hands, and arms, and feet and legs get heavier and heavier, your body is filled with wonderful PEACE. You are serene, utterly at rest, utterly at PEACE. You are filled with quietness and confidence. You have let go, and you are being filled with the PEACE that is beyond all human understanding.

The fourth word is *DEEPER!* You need to become still more DEEPLY released from your body. Count silently from one to five along with me. With every count, your body will get more and more inert, more and more relaxed, and limp, and peaceful. Count silently now: one—deeper; two—deeper and deeper; three—*deep*er, and *deep*er, and *deep*er; four—*s t i l l d e e p e r*; five—DEEPER yet—into the deepest, fullest peace and inertness your body has ever achieved. But your conscious mind is still alert. Your spirit feels free, and light, and poised.

Concentration also is indispensable

If the preliminary preparation is achieved, it brings you into close harmony and partnership with superhuman power. You are then ready for the next step—concentration. To shut out all wandering thoughts, all ideas and interests except the main problem that has brought you into the presence of God, is the objective. Paul said: "This one thing I do." This step means: "On this one thing I center now all my thought, all my attention, all my seeking."

Here is the crucial step in deep prayer for courage

All the preliminaries have now been set forth. If you have followed these suggestions through, step by step, you are at this stage seated in a dark, quiet place, in a state of profound relaxation, and yet of dedication and concentration. If this has been achieved, you are ready for deep prayer.

In this Presence, facing whatever it is that seems to menace and damage your personality and your purpose, you are ready to pray, silently:

"Come what may, O God, under Thy guidance,
and by Thy power, we will go forward with courage,
with joy, and with creative love. Amen!"

At this point comes a miracle

Miracles are *not* events contrary to natural law, events that cannot happen. Rather, a miracle is the scientifically lawful operation of spiritual power and wisdom when it comes into action on the material, biological, psychological or social levels of reality.

If you have been able to carry out fully and effectively the steps suggested in the preceding pages, you will have achieved a condition in which spiritual power will flood into your mind, your heart, and your body. Your depression will be gone. You will "be of good courage." "He will strengthen your heart."

You will emerge from your prayer, filled with the peace that passes all understanding, and ready to go forward into your daily work with energy, enthusiasm, and creative friendliness. The gloom that may have been shadowing you will be gone. With the help of God, the energies of your whole being, both conscious and unconscious, will have been redirected into channels where they will be creative instead of destructive.

FOLLOWING UP THE MIRACLE

Let the joy sink in!

Through deep prayer, you have reached a profound assurance that the love of God surrounds you, and guards you, and leads you on. You will understand what the poet meant when he wrote: "I only know I cannot drift beyond His love and care." And you will understand what the Psalmist meant, thousands of years earlier, when he said:

If I make my bed in Hell, behold Thou art there.
If I take the wings of the morning,
And dwell in the uttermost part of the sea,
Even there shall Thy hand lead me,
And thy right hand shall hold me.

But over and above that calm assurance is the new tide of courage and of power that swells up in the heart out of deep prayer. Sensing this surge of joy and of creative love, let us worship and bow down. Let us render to Him our heartfelt thanks. Then, in our new-found courage, let us go forward!

By pulling and by letting go

An ancient papyrus contains the words:

The archer hits the target by pulling and by letting go;
The boatman reaches the harbor by pulling and by letting go.

The man at the oars, rowing toward his home harbor, may be taken to represent the spiritual adventurer. Deep prayer is the pause between struggles in the outer world. You have "let go, and let God." But now, in your deep prayer, you have found new strength, courage, and faith. The time has come to plunge your oar-blades back into the tide once more, and to put your back joyously into the tug that will send you and your craft forward toward your great objective.

Repeat as needed!

Once you have experienced the deliverance out of the Slough of Despond—the lifting of your spirit out of the Valley of the Shadow—you will have realized, for a moment, the power of deep prayer. But most of us are prone to forget. We slip back into the habit of living in the mood of the moment. Before we know it, we slump down from the hills of light into the gloom once more. And once we have let discouragement take hold of us again, it is hard to believe that the upsurge of joy and courage that once came out of deep prayer were real.

School yourself to *act* as if it were possible to attain it again. Test it out once more, and prove to yourself that unbounded sources of courage and of joy *are* available, whenever we are willing to ask, and seek, and knock at the door.

Are there limits?

No matter what problem you face, life will be richer if you make the best of it rather than the worst of it. To grapple courageously and cooperate creatively are always wiser than to acquiesce ignobly, to evade cravenly, and to attack vindictively. Courage and creative cooperation are basic ways of making the best of whatever seemingly menacing situation you may confront.

But are there limits to the extent to which any given person can achieve courage, by even the most thorough and determined use of deep prayer? Let us suppose that someone is married to a basically cruel and unscrupulous mate, who takes advantage of every generous act, and who systematically meets kindness and affection with betrayal. If the friendliness and creative cooperation, achieved through prayer, have been rebuffed and used with ruthless selfishness time after time, the attainment of new friendliness may become more and more difficult.

Or let us suppose that one has dedicated years to writing a book or building up a business, or to some other creative effort, and let us suppose that the book proves to be unsaleable to any publisher, or that the business sinks deeper and deeper into financial loss. If failure is repeated too often, the regaining of courage may seem to be a psychological impossibility.

Can prayer succeed, even in such extreme cases? The answer to that is wrapped up in another question: How fully are you willing to test the hypothesis that God's love, with unlimited power and wisdom, seeks fulfillment of life for you and for all mankind? If you are willing to go the whole distance, there is always an answer. If you are willing to stake your very life and all that you hold dear upon the goodness of God, and if, in that dedication, you will faithfully make full use of listening prayer and of deep prayer, you will find the upward road of spiritual blessing and of rich service.

When we experience failure, that means that what has happened does not fulfill that on which we set our hearts. To become discouraged is to put the blame upon what *happened*. But perhaps our *purposes* have been wrong. Go back to your dedication. Seek humbly and openheartedly to discover what spiritual goals God really sets before you. Realign your life to the purposes that listening prayer illuminates. Then failure disappears. The glory of living the spiritual life comes surging back.

TO SUM UP

All of us have faltered, more or less, in the great task of living courageously and creatively. These failures of ours have been due to our misuses of emotional energy.

Common sense can help greatly in our search for courage if we

take an inventory of the menace;
let possible lines of action become clear; and
pour all our energy into taking the best available road.

But deep prayer can lift this process up to new high levels.

The miracle of finding spiritual power to solve daily problems can be achieved if we fully practice reconciliation, isolation, invocation, dedication, relaxation, and concentration. Then the prayer for courage brings the surge of power, friendliness and joy.

Once achieved, we need to

drink in the glory of it;
apply the newly empowered courage in daily living; and
repeat the process whenever the need comes.

The courage that deep prayer can give need be limited only by the limits of our willingness.

Chapter 8

Prayer Can Change Enmity
Into Friendliness

BROTHERLY LOVE HAS BEEN A MAGNIFICENT ASPIRATION

Reconciliation and dedication are the keys

For full success in the use of listening prayer and deep prayer, reconciliation to one another and dedication to fulfillment of life for all are needed. Let us suppose that there is a group of people in which more and more of the members live up to these ideals more and more wholeheartedly. What will happen? No member will hold resentment, antagonism or enmity against any outsider. Each member will be wholeheartedly dedicated to promoting, both in the group and universally, the brotherhood of mankind, the world-wide Kingdom of Heaven on earth that was dreamed of by the Hebrew prophets, and which was preached by Jesus.

Heaven may be defined as a social and spiritual state in which everyone, freely and joyously, works cooperatively for

94

the common good. Such a group of people would, by definition, be a little segment of heaven on earth.

The early Christians reached toward such an achievement

Many passages in the New Testament suggest that what Jesus was seeking to inspire his disciples to do was to go out and found units of such a Beloved Community on earth, with the knowledge that these communities would have within them the germ of power to grow and to multiply, as the cells of yeast multiply and leaven a lump of dough, or as cells in a mustard seed grow, divide, and multiply until the result is a spreading structure of life and beauty. That the radiant joy of such communities of brotherly love was realized at times, and within limits, is suggested by various passages in the Book of Acts and in the Epistles which make up the remainder of the New Testament, and by episodes in the history of the early Church.

The great founder and promoter of such communities during the first century of the Christian Era was the Apostle Paul. In the twelfth chapter of Romans, he set down, in radiantly simple and concrete terms, some of the fundamentals on which such communities of shared life and brotherly love must be built. The following is the text of that chapter: *

THE APOSTLE PAUL'S RULES FOR LIVING
THE BROTHERLY LIFE

The dedication

Well, then, my brothers, I appeal to you by all the mercy of God to dedicate your bodies as a living sacrifice, consecrated and acceptable to God; that is your cult, a spiritual rite. Instead of being moulded to this world, have your mind renewed, and so be transformed in nature, able to make out what the will of God is, namely, what is good and acceptable to Him and perfect.

---

* As translated by Moffatt, but freely rearranged and with inserted headings.

The brotherly community

Keep in harmony with one another; instead of being ambitious, associate with humble folk; never be
selfish.

In virtue of my office, I tell everyone of your number who is self-important, that he is not to think more
of himself than he ought to think; he must take a sane
view of himself, corresponding to the degree of faith
that God has assigned to each. In our one body we
have a number of members, and the members have
not all the same function; so, too, for all our numbers, we form one Body in Christ and we are severally
members one of another. Our talents differ with the
grace that is given us; if the talent is that of prophecy,
let us employ it in proportion to our faith; if it is
practical service, let us mind our service; the teacher
must mind his teaching, the speaker his words of coun-
sel; the contributor must be liberal, the superintend-
ent must be in earnest, the sick visitor must be cheerful.

Some practical applications of the law of love

Let your love be a real thing, with a loathing for
evil and a bent for what is good. Put affection into
your love for the brotherhood; be forward to honor
one another; never let your zeal flag; maintain the
spiritual glow; serve the Lord; let your hope be a
joy to you; be steadfast in trouble, attend to prayer,
contribute to needy saints, make a practice of hospital-
ity. Rejoice with those who rejoice, and weep with
those who weep.

What to do about those who fail to love

Bless those who make a practice of persecuting you;
bless them instead of cursing them. Never pay back
evil for evil; aim to be above reproach in the eyes of
all; be at peace with all men, if possible, so far as
that depends on you. Never revenge yourselves, be-

loved, but let the wrath of God have its way; for it is written, Vengeance is mine, I will exact a requital— the Lord has said it. No, if your enemy is hungry, feed him, if he is thirsty, give him drink; for in this way you will make him feel a burning sense of shame.

Do not let evil get the better of you; get the better of evil by doing good.

THE GREAT RELIGIONS, AND WORLD BROTHERHOOD

The vision of the Kingdom of God (or, as someone has called it, the Family of God) has usually been regarded by Christians as a unique contribution by Jesus to the thought and aspirations of mankind. But the Christian ideals in this respect grew up out of similar aspirations that appeared in the Jewish Scriptures of the Old Testament:

> Thou shalt love thy neighbor as thyself. Love ye the stranger; for, ye were strangers. Loosen all that fetters men unfairly. Share your food with hungry men, and take the homeless to your home. Clothe the naked when ye see them, and never turn from any fellow creature.

Parallel passages are to be found in the scriptures of various other religions, including Buddhism, Jainism, and Hinduism.

Three hundred years before Christ, Zeno founded Stoicism, of which Gilbert Murray has written in his book, *The Five Stages of Greek Religion:*

> Many kings and great Roman governors professed Stoicism. It held before them the ideal of universal brotherhood, and of duty to the "Great Society of Gods and Men"; it enabled them to work, indifferent to mere pain and pleasure, as servants of the divine purpose and "fellow-workers with God" in building up a human Cosmos within the eternal Cosmos.

Dedicated individuals already belong to the

Beloved Community

When any human being gives himself unreservedly to the service of love, of truth, and of ideal justice, he becomes a nucleus of the universal brotherhood. He no longer seeks to exploit his fellows or to domineer over them. He is eager only to understand them, to learn from them, to aid them in their own highest aspirations, and to establish creative fellowship with them.

This individual may be imperfectly dedicated. He may blunder and fall short. Yet if he persists in his devotion, and if he keeps redirecting his course toward the goal of truth and brotherly love whenever he finds that he has deviated, he will embody more and more fully the great ideal. Though he himself should be overwhelmed and destroyed, his vision, once set forth, will take possession of other people. The brotherhood will spread. The Beloved Community will increasingly come into being.

HOW PRAYER CAN TURN THESE IDEALS
INTO REALITIES

We have already seen that the first steps in listening prayer, and also in deep prayer, are for the purpose of bringing the worshipper into harmony with the Fatherly Love of God and with the brotherly love which is inseparable from recognition of that Fatherhood. These steps, in their deep essence, cannot be left out if the power of prayer is to be invoked. Having established this attitude of love and partnership, you are ready to employ deep prayer for the purpose of changing enmity into friendliness. We need this kind of prayer every time we feel any sense of resentment, bitterness, antagonism, reproachfulness, or unfriendliness toward any human being with whom our lives have contact. Indeed, this form of prayer may be thought of as a further development of reconciliation.

Whether the object of your prayer is then a person toward

whom you might apply Christ's command to love your enemies, or whether it is your deeply beloved life partner or son or daughter or friend, call up in your mind as vivid a mental image as you can summon of this one toward whom your deep prayer is now to be directed.

Build inwardly the triangle of brotherly prayer

In your profound relaxation, think of yourself as being the near, lower corner of the triangle. Think of your would-be

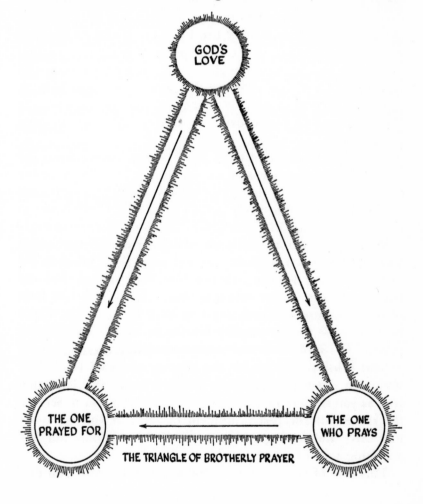

GOD'S LOVE

THE ONE PRAYED FOR

THE ONE WHO PRAYS

THE TRIANGLE OF BROTHERLY PRAYER

enemy (or the blundering and troublesome person—or the loved one—for whom you want to pray) as being at the other lower corner. Think of an open channel extending from you to this person whom you have thus inwardly visualized. Think of this channel as being the lower side of a great triangle that you are to build in your inner mind.

Now, bring into your consciousness an awareness of the love of God. Think of that love as a center of shining power blazing high above you and above the person for whom you are about to pray. According to the Old Testament story, the Children of Israel were led through the wilderness by a pillar of cloud by day and a pillar of fire by night. Think of the love of God as something akin to that pillar of fire.

The far side of the triangle extends downward from this blazing center of God's love to the person for whom you are to pray. The near side of the triangle stretches down from the blazing center of God's love to you as you sit here in deep meditation.

Now begin to think of the love of God streaming down the far side of the triangle and surrounding with shining power this person for whom you desire to pray. God's love surrounds him and enfolds him. With radiant good will, God's power is ready to make his life wonderful. The love of God ardently seeks that this person shall find fulfillment of life. God wants him to achieve rich, abundant, and creative living. God, as the perfectly loving Father, will not force this person. But the power of God's love is enfolding him, ready to be laid hold of whenever this person is ready to avail himself of it. God's love seeks the highest possible fulfillment for the one you are praying for, subject to that person's own free decision.

Now think of the ardent and shining power of God's love streaming down the near side of the triangle and enfolding you, as you sit here in prayer. God's love wants you to achieve the richest and deepest fulfillment of life that you are ready to receive and willing to accept. God's love enfolds you like a shining wall of creative power.

This love of God enfolding you is infinitely great. You cannot possibly use it all. As you accept His love you find that its abundance overflows. God's love surges out across the lower side, through the channel that forms the base of the triangle of brotherly prayer. Think of this shining power streaming across the base of the triangle and merging with the love that comes down directly from God toward the one for whom you are praying.

The two streams of love unite around him, seeking his fulfillment, eager to aid his every good aspiration and purpose.

Hold in your mind for a while this fiery triangle of love, good will, and creative power. Hold, for at least five minutes, if you can, the vision of it surrounding you and surrounding your friend.

Use prayer to prepare friendly reactions

After you have spent five minutes meditating on the triangle of brotherly prayer, you may be ready to come out of your deep relaxation. Before you do so, use this form of prayer:

O God, prompted by Thy Spirit, whenever this person seems to be irritating or damaging, that will remind me to respond with understanding and with friendliness.

Repeat that prayer once or twice silently to yourself. Then come out of your deep relaxation and go on about your work or your recreation.

Using the three "—ates" in prayer

In most of our human relationships, what we can do for our associates can be summed up quite well in three words ending with the syllable "ate": *stimulate, liberate,* and *facilitate.* There is a fourth "—ate"—*integrate;* but most people have to take the responsibility for doing that themselves.

To stimulate other people is possible by asking the right kinds of interested questions, by being a good listener, by helping to bring the person into life-stirring contacts, all these, of course, if, as, and when the person shows interested responses to our friendly outreachings.

To liberate our associates, to help to set them free, is one of the really great services we can render. Quite often what we need to do is to make them free from restrictions and hamperings that we ourselves have imposed.

And then, we can almost always do things that will facilitate: we can observe understandingly what are the aspirations, the hopes, the creative outreachings of this other person, and then we may be able to discover ways in which we can supply resources needed to make it possible for those good dreams to come true. Sometimes encouragement is what is needed to facilitate. Sometimes willingness to do what the other person asks us to do is the needed facilitation.

Card-playing and religion have not always been in harmony with one another. But bridge players have an expression that fits into the picture at this point: "Lead into your partner's long suit." From the theatre comes another helpful expression of this sort: "Set the stage for the other person." These two sayings fit together with another well-worn observation:

> Most of us spend our energy trying to make other people good and ourselves happy; but what would really contribute to joyous living would be if we tried to make ourselves good and other people happy.

When you enter into your corner of the triangle of meditation, and begin to see God's love streaming down toward the person with whom you wish to achieve friendliness, you may begin to see ways in which you can stimulate, liberate, and facilitate him. Focus your full attention for a few minutes on just how these achievements might work out. Get the constructive picture clearly in your mind. Then thank God for it, and when you next meet the person, remember those three "—ates."

Putting inspiration into action

When Jesus explained the meaning of "Thou shalt love thy neighbor as thyself" in terms of the parable of the Good Samaritan, he stressed action rather than words. Brotherly prayer will change unconscious as well as conscious attitudes. But attitudes are of very little significance unless and until they bring about action.

The love of God has miracle-working power

The spiritual seeker needs to understand the nature of miracles. A miracle is not a violation of the laws of nature. Any such idea is self-contradictory, for the laws of nature are simply descriptions of the ways in which reality acts and operates. In a very real sense, there can be nothing supernatural, for natural law operates in the spiritual world as well as in the world of physics, chemistry, and biology. But we must realize that above the four levels recognized by science—the material, the biological, the psychological, and the sociological—there is a fifth level of reality—namely, the spiritual. This is the level on which superhuman power and wisdom operate.

When spiritual forces come into the physical, biological, psychological, and sociological realms of reality, and produce effects there, we may well call such operations miraculous. In this sense, to be truly inspired and guided by God is a veritable miracle. To be freed from emotional depression and discouragement by the inflow of faith and the baptism of God's love and courage is a miracle.

The miraculous change in you

Meditation on the triangle of brotherly prayer can, in this sense, work miracles. If you carry out faithfully the steps described above, you will find first that your own attitudes begin to change. As you think of your friend who has a problem as being surrounded by the love of God, you yourself begin to

understand him better. You begin to ask: "What problems and
difficulties may be making him act the way he has been acting? How could the things that irritate and hurt him be re-
moved? How could I act towards him in a way which would
make our relationship creative instead of destructive?"

Not only do ideas come in answer to such questions, but
powerful changes take place also in your conscious and unconscious attitudes. You will find that you actually begin to feel
friendly toward this person. You will find that forgiveness is
easy—forgiveness in the sense of dissolving and removing whatever barriers your resentment has raised against partnership
between you two in working for good results.

Changes appear also in the problem person

Those who have tried this form of brotherly prayer report
that something else seems to happen. The person for whom
they have been praying seems to be changed. His irritating
and unjust behavior seems to disappear, or to be reduced. He
seems to become more friendly, more cooperative, more understanding.

Perhaps you will have to repeat this form of prayer several
times—even day after day. But if you will persist in it, you will
find that the relationship changes rapidly for the better.

IN THIS CASE, THE TRIANGLE OF MEDITATION
TURNED DISASTER INTO TRIUMPH

A graduate student, whom we will call Rudolf X. Smith, was
struggling to produce an acceptable thesis, which was required
before he could be awarded a Ph.D. degree. The degree was
vitally important to him because he needed it in order to se-
cure the kind of teaching position to which he aspired.

Rudolf had had a long, struggling climb up to this point at
which his degree seemed almost within his grasp. As a school-
boy he had witnessed violent quarrels between his father and
mother, ending in a divorce in which his custody was awarded
to his mother, though he secretly believed that she was the one

who was to blame. His mother soon married again. Rudolf's stepfather was sharply critical of the boy and continually scolded and punished him.

As a result of these experiences, Rudolf retreated within himself. As much as possible he avoided the company of other people, and when he was with a group, he hardly spoke a word.

But inwardly he felt the stirrings of the ambition to be somebody. Driven from home by his stepfather's antagonism, he took a job at a factory and supported himself. Under pressure, he joined the union, whose meetings he attended silently but observantly. The antagonisms and conflicts between labor and management and between rival leaders in the union impressed him as wasteful and damaging to all concerned. He resolved to get more education so that he might be able to do something effective about labor relations.

His grades in school had been excellent. Before starting his work in the factory, he had, at the age of sixteen, completed high school. Now, spurred by his new ambition, he went to evening school every night in the week, and completed his work for a college degree in an amazingly short time. His academic record was so good that he was awarded an assistantship in the Sociology Department of Duke University. He specialized in industrial sociology.

He found his courses absorbingly interesting. But the thing that fascinated him most was the field work that he undertook, under the direction of one of his professors. In this survey he gathered hundreds of case studies of industrial disputes.

The professor who was directing his thesis was a very strong-willed man. He had dogmatic ideas about just how the cases should be recorded, and just how the statistical tables should be worked out. Rudolf felt serious doubts, but he knew that he had to get this professor's approval if he wanted to win his degree.

Rudolf's assistantship had been renewed for a second year. Since the rules forbade awarding the assistantship for a third year, Rudolf accepted a part-time instructorship, teaching Introductory Sociology to a large class of sophomores. The salary was barely enough to live on, but Rudolf was determined to attain his objective.

Finally, the case studies were completed. The supervising professor insisted on putting the data into literally hundreds of statistical tables. Rudolf wanted to have these tables approved by other members of the committee who were to examine him on his thesis, but the professor insisted on having the work typed up immediately, in the elaborate form required by the university, at a cost of $150. At this point the supervising professor turned the manuscript of the thesis over to the head of the department for approval. When the department head saw the mass of statistics he had an emotional explosion. He told Rudolf: "These tables are completely meaningless!"

At this stage, Rudolf brought the pile of manuscript into my office. He said to me:

> I'm at the end of my rope! I have paid for the typing but now I have no money to eat with. I see no hope of getting the professors to agree about my thesis. I've done exactly what I was told to do (even when I disagreed with the directing professor), but now the professors are fighting each other.
>
> I know it's a cowardly thing to do, but the whole thing is completely hopeless. I am going to resign my instructorship, leave the university, and find some sort of job to keep me alive.
>
> But actually I'd rather be dead! I don't see any use in trying to go on. These years of struggle have landed me in an impasse. I don't really know why I'm bothering you about it. I just want to quit. I'd be better off if I quit life itself!

When Rudolf thus told me of his despair, I already had my hands full of responsibilities that crowded every hour. When I looked at the costly statistical tables I felt sure that they were quite unacceptable. They violated rule after rule of statistics. The student's attitude of resentment, self-pity, and despair seemed to provide little basis for constructive effort.

But I believed in the power of deep prayer. I myself, by

using deep prayer, had been rescued from disasters as threatening and appalling as those that the student faced. I looked at Rudolf silently for a full minute. Then I said: "Mr. Smith, you seem to be facing a very menacing situation. It seems to you to threaten complete disaster. But let me ask you one question: 'Do you propose to make the worst of this situation? Or do you propose to seek the ways by which you can make the best of it?' "

Rudolf did not answer. He sat there looking at me glumly. Then I said: "About how you're going to eat until the next pay day—you know that there is a student loan fund. I feel sure that you can get enough there to keep you going."

"Oh, I can't do that," Rudolf protested. "I'd lie awake all night worrying about being in debt!"

"Well," I said, "leave your thesis with me overnight, and come back tomorrow."

I put my other work aside and began to study the thesis and the voluminous pile of tables. As the manuscript stood, it seemed perfectly clear that no one on the examining committee would vote for the thesis except the professor who had directed it. The antagonism between the directing professor, the head of the department, and Rudolf seemed to create a quite hopeless impasse.

So I took the problem home with me. And in the quiet of the night, I entered into deep prayer, using the triangle. I envisioned Rudolf Smith at the opposite lower corner of the triangle, with myself at the other lower corner. Then I envisioned the power and the love of God shining radiantly at the apex of the triangle, and streaming down the two sides, enveloping Rudolf with serene aspiration for fulfillment of his life, encompassing me also with the same creative power, and streaming from me across the bottom of the triangle to reinforce the creative love that was surrounding Rudolf.

Holding this shining triangle clearly in my mind, I thought of the supervising professor as being at the far corner of a second triangle, and the head of the department being at the far corner of a third triangle, with lines connecting each of

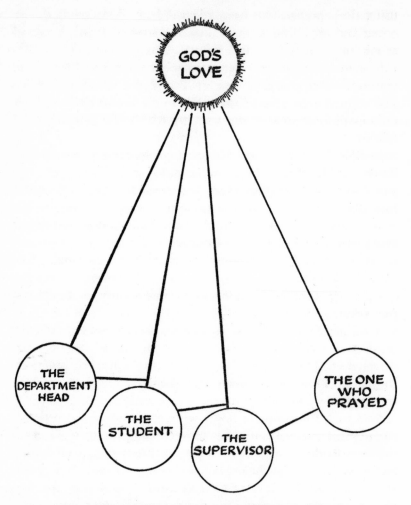

TRIANGLES OF BROTHERLY PRAYER FOR THREE PEOPLE

them to Rudolf and to me. Down to all the lower angles of
the triangles I envisioned the love and power of God streaming with its creative potential.

As I sat thus in deep prayer, the problem began to clarify
itself. I realized, first, that the case materials which Rudolf
had collected had a vast amount of real value. No one had
gathered just this kind of records before. The cases had been
studied with care, and the facts had been recorded with meticu-
lous patience. The thing that was needed was to bring out

the actual results of the study in a form which could be accepted by the social scientists who had to pass judgment on the thesis.

Next morning I wrote out a brief memorandum that stated the impossibility of accepting the thesis as it stood, but which also showed that a good thesis could be achieved by certain rather arduous steps of revision. I took a copy of this memorandum to the head of the department. After an hour of discussion we agreed substantially that Rudolf could still win success by the right kind of hard work.

A copy of the memorandum was given to Rudolf. I said to him: "Mr. Smith, the choice between success and failure lies in your hands. If you can find a way to rework the statistics along the lines that I have indicated, I believe your thesis can be accepted."

Within two hours Rudolf was back. He said: "All right; I'm going to try it. What do I do first? And how do I get the approval of my directing professor?"

A solution to that problem also was found by using the triangle of brotherly love. Rudolf won his degree—with special commendation for the creative contribution that his thesis made to better industrial relations. The directing professor received full credit for the creative courage that had launched the project, and that had carried it up to within reach of successful completion. Among us three professors, and between us and the student, a new bond of friendly understanding and loyalty had resulted. And Rudolf told me that the working out of this crisis had been one of the greatest turning points in his life. Prayer can work wonders!

WHERE YOU CAN APPLY BROTHERLY PRAYER

In describing this method of turning enmity into friendliness, the problem person has been presented, in general, as anyone who irritates or injures the one who is to pray. But it will help us to make fuller and more effective use of this form of prayer if we name off briefly at least some of the particular situations in which this spiritual exercise is needed.

1. Husbands and wives will find this a fundamental help,

in removing friction from their marriage and in building up higher and higher levels of joyous love.

2. Parents in their dealings with their children, and children in their dealings with their parents, will find this form of prayer a vital aid.

3. Students attending boarding schools and colleges will find this a help in getting rid of the friction that so often arises between roommates. Students will also find it desirable to use this form of prayer in improving their own attitudes toward those professors and instructors who seem to them to be unjust, overbearing, or otherwise unreasonable.

4. Neighbors who get irritated with their neighbors need to use this form of prayer.

5. Workers in offices, stores, or factories need to use brotherly prayer in dealing with the enmities, the suspicions, the resentments, and the other antagonisms that so often breed hatred where friendly partnership should prevail.

THE CHURCH AND THE BELOVED COMMUNITY

A new world order based on social justice and on brotherly love has been the vision proclaimed by the Hebrew prophets of old, by Jesus of Nazareth, and by many of the most inspired leaders of the Church. Jesus referred to it most often as the Kingdom of God. In the Gospel according to Matthew, it is frequently called the Kingdom of Heaven. Some modern thinkers have called it the Family of God. Josiah Royce called it the Beloved Community.

But, by whatever name it is called, these things are clear: This Beloved Community was to spread by the process of cellular multiplication—like the growth of a mustard seed to a spreading plant, or like the way in which the cells of yeast permeate a batch of dough. The spirit of brotherly love was to be contagious; it was to spread from person to person, in wider and wider areas of loving cooperation.

Now the Church has been referred to as the embodiment of the Spirit of Christ. Ideally, churches are formed by the coming together of personalities who have been transformed by contagion of the spirit of love, and who aid and strengthen one another in the practice of the life of love, guided by the Spirit of God.

These facts challenge the Church with a supreme test. If the Christian religion is effective in achieving the ideals that it proclaims, then churches should be shining examples of the Beloved Community. In these fellowships, anyone who seeks to learn more of the life of the spirit and to express more admirably the life of love should find himself supported, encouraged, aided, and inspired by his fellow members and by the leaders of the church. We are confronted therefore by a performance test. How well do we live up to our ideals?

THESE, THEN, ARE THE ESSENTIAL STEPS IN DEEP PRAYER FOR TURNING ENMITY INTO FRIENDLINESS

The creation of communities of brotherly love has been a magnificent aspiration

Reconciliation and dedication are keys to heaven on earth.

The Apostle Paul stated clearly and simply some basic rules for living the brotherly life.

Not only Christianity, but also other religions lay stress on the vital importance of brotherly love.

Wherever dedicated individuals are loyal to the ideal, the Beloved Community has begun to come into being.

Deep prayer can turn these ideals into realities

The first steps are the same as in prayer for courage.
The triangle of brotherly prayer brings God's love to bear.
Miraculous changes result.
Brotherly prayer is applicable in all social relations.

The Church should be an organized embodiment of the Beloved Community

$$\overline{\text{O}\text{II}\text{O}\text{II}\text{O}\text{II}\text{O}\text{II}\text{O}\text{II}\text{O}\text{II}\text{O}\text{II}\text{O}\text{II}\text{O}\text{II}\text{O}\text{II}\text{O}\text{II}\text{O}\text{II}\text{O}\text{II}\text{O}\text{II}\text{O}\text{II}\text{O}\text{II}\text{O}\text{II}\text{O}}$$

Howto Conquer

Temptation by Prayer

WHAT IS TEMPTATION?

As far back as the records of religion go, men have been struggling against temptation. But what is temptation? Traditional discussions have defined it in terms of dogmas and taboos. Many a modern mind no longer finds such terms acceptable, yet temptation is certainly a very real thing for almost all of us. What is its actual meaning in terms of the values that an intelligent, modern-minded person can accept?

Fundamentally:

Temptation means the urge to get what we want, by methods that are likely to damage ourselves or others in the long run. If that is a good definition, then the only way in which we can understand temptation—and really come to grips with it—is to find a clear answer to a previous question—namely, this:

What do you and I really want out of life?

This whole world of ours is teeming with human beings who struggle, strive, aspire, hope, and desire. You and I are among them. People labor and toil to get money, and then rush out and spend it. People set up programs for daily activities, and send surges of energy into their muscles in the endeavors to carry out those programs. People press down the accelerators of their cars, and bend over the steering wheels, rushing through congested highway traffic, trying to get places so as to do things.

But what things? And why? What is the purpose of all this striving? What do we *really* want to experience and to achieve?

Can you put it in a formula?

Can you and I state in clear and useful words the goals of our striving, so that we may more wisely and with more triumphant success achieve the victories which actually, in our deepest hearts, we long to achieve? Yes, there is such a basic formula:

You and I want to live vividly. We want to live richly. We want to gather in the harvest of deep, and intense, and satisfying experiences. Life fulfillment includes wholesome thrills. The goal of religion (as has been pointed out in Chapter 2 of this book) is fulfillment of life. Jesus said that he had come that men might live life to the full. Now fulfillment of life certainly includes having intense, vivid, memorable experiences, and having them on the five levels of personality—material, biological, psychological, sociological, and spiritual. To sum up this need for intensely satisfying experiences, let us draw a horizontal line with a plus-sign at the right-hand end and a minus-sign at the left-hand end, thus:

PAIN NOW, AND	JOY
− FRUSTRATION	NOW +

Every normal human being wants to move toward the plus end, and away from the minus end of this dimension of vivid living. Everybody wants to have "joy now." Everybody wants to avoid "pain and frustration now." All the rich splendor of joy-now belongs over toward the right-hand end of this horizontal dimension.

Life ought to be thrilling, not every moment, but certainly very often and very deeply. Your work should be thrilling. Your family life should very often be thrilling. Your love should bring thrills. Play should be rich with thrills. Yes, life ought to be thrilling at times—and at other times it ought to be restful, peaceful, and reassuring. All normal people accept this basic goal of joy now, of living richly and fully over toward the right-hand end of this horizontal dimension. This is a normal part of fulfillment of life. But thrills-now are not the whole story. There is another dimension to consider.

Thrills may mean smash-ups

Do you like to sit behind the steering wheel of a powerful car and really burn up the road? Do you like to step on the accelerator until the telephone poles seem to just whiz past your ears? Perhaps you do not go quite to that extreme, but a great many people get an intensely vivid experience out of speeding a powerful car down a ribbon of concrete.

Let us suppose that a speeder is doing that right now. The girl he is in love with is sitting beside him. He sees a big red barn about a tenth of a mile down the hill on his right, with an orchard and a stone wall across the road on the left. He does not know it, but just behind that barn and that orchard there is another ribbon of concrete intersecting his. Down that other road is coming another driver who is getting an intense thrill out of speed. The first driver's career intersects the second driver's career right down by that barn. When that first driver comes back to consciousness (if he ever does) he is likely to find himself looking up in a hazy sort of way at a man in white who is bending over him. Then we can imagine our driver asking:

"Doctor, what's the matter with my legs?"

"Oh," the doctor replies, "we had to put them in plaster casts."

"But, doctor," the speeder asks, "how long will I have to wear these casts?"

"We hope not more than two months."

"Doctor," the speeder persists, "will I be able to walk, run, swim, and dance when you take the casts off?"

"Well, maybe!" the doctor answers soberly.

This smash-up illustrates the basic difficulty in thrills as a means of finding fulfillment of life. Some thrills, like reckless speeding, carry with them menacing risks of tearing down structures needed for future joy. In his collision, our imaginary driver smashed up not only the structures of the bones in his legs, but also the structure of his car, the structure of his plans and his peace of mind, and the structure of his social relationships. Quite possibly it also created in him a deep sense of guilt. And the sweetheart who was snuggling so trustingly up against him—her shattered body lay down in the morgue. Just before the crash, this imaginary driver was having plenty of "joy now." But instead of gaining fulfillment of life through that joy, he swiftly discovered that he had bought his thrills at the cost of finding himself wrecked, crushed, and agonized.

The vertical dimension of the plus-plus diagram

Because of the facts just pointed out, we need to add a second dimension to the one shown above. When this is done, we get the diagram that appears on the following page. Note that this vertical dimension has a plus sign at the top and a minus sign at the bottom. Just below the plus sign are the words "Build Up." Just above the minus sign are the words "Tear Down." Build up what? Why, build up the structures needed for future joy. That is what happens when your activities are near the top of this vertical dimension. But if they are near the bottom of that dimension, then those activities are tearing down the structures needed for future joy.

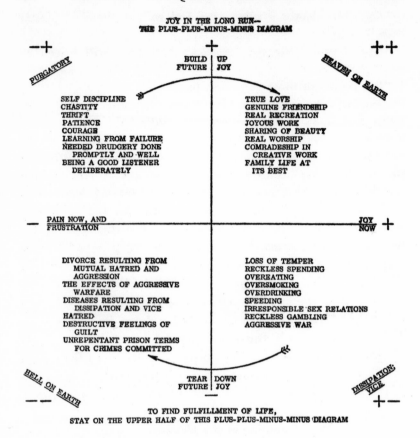

JOY IN THE LONG RUN—
THE PLUS-PLUS-MINUS-MINUS DIAGRAM

−+   +   ++

PURGATORY

BUILD | UP
FUTURE | JOY

HEAVEN ON EARTH

SELF DISCIPLINE
CHASTITY
THRIFT
PATIENCE
COURAGE
LEARNING FROM FAILURE
NEEDED DRUDGERY DONE
  PROMPTLY AND WELL
BEING A GOOD LISTENER
  DELIBERATELY

TRUE LOVE
GENUINE FRIENDSHIP
REAL RECREATION
JOYOUS WORK
SHARING OF BEAUTY
REAL WORSHIP
COMRADESHIP IN
  CREATIVE WORK
FAMILY LIFE AT
  ITS BEST

−   PAIN NOW, AND
     FRUSTRATION

JOY
NOW   +

DIVORCE RESULTING FROM
  MUTUAL HATRED AND
  AGGRESSION
THE EFFECTS OF AGGRESSIVE
  WARFARE
DISEASES RESULTING FROM
  DISSIPATION AND VICE
HATRED
DESTRUCTIVE FEELINGS OF
  GUILT
UNREPENTANT PRISON TERMS
  FOR CRIMES COMMITTED

LOSS OF TEMPER
RECKLESS SPENDING
OVEREATING
OVERSMOKING
OVERDRINKING
SPEEDING
IRRESPONSIBLE SEX RELATIONS
RECKLESS GAMBLING
AGGRESSIVE WAR

HELL ON EARTH

TEAR | DOWN
FUTURE | JOY

DISSIPATION;
VICE

−−   +−

TO FIND FULFILLMENT OF LIFE,
STAY ON THE UPPER HALF OF THIS PLUS-PLUS-MINUS-MINUS DIAGRAM

OUR TWO DIMENSIONS THUS GIVE US FOUR QUARTERS

In the upper right-hand region we have:

The plus-plus quarter

In this quarter belongs any and every activity that does both of two things: it belongs here if it brings joy-now and if at the same time it builds up the structures needed for future joy.

To illustrate, true love belongs in the plus-plus quarter. True love brings deep and intense joy-now. True love is also creative. It is one of the most creative experiences that can come to any human being. When two people love each other they begin to build dreams together. When they get married, those dreams take physical embodiment in the form of the home in which they start their married life. Their love inspires them to acquire furniture, to beautify their grounds, to create the surroundings in which life can be lived joyously and lovingly. And then, normally, true love brings into the world the miracle of children. True love certainly belongs up toward the top of the vertical dimension. So we find it here in the plus-plus quarter. True love is good.

Real recreation also belongs in the plus-plus quarter. Another thing that belongs here is joyous work. The creation and the sharing of beauty belong here. And the rapture of true worship—for those fully initiated into it—may be in the very highest reaches of this plus-plus quarter. Anything that belongs in this quarter is a help toward fulfillment of life. Therefore, any such thing is *good*.

If all your activities could be carried out in the plus-plus quarter, you would be joyous the whole time. You would spend much of your efforts working with comrades and partners, freely and joyously for the common good. That would be "heaven on earth"—and you will note that that is how this quarter is labeled.

Down in the lower right-hand region of our chart we find

The plus-minus quarter

This is the quarter containing all the activities that start out plus and end up minus. Activities in this quarter start in joy and end in pain. Here belong all the activities that bring thrills at first, but that tend to tear down structures needed for future joy.

We have already explored the case of reckless speeding. Certainly that belongs here in the plus-minus quarter.

As a second possible candidate for this quarter, let me ask how you feel about gambling. It certainly is one of the very thrilling sorts of experience. Let us say simply that in so far as this kind of thrill results in tearing down the structures needed for future joy, it belongs in the plus-minus quarter. Our goal is fulfillment of life. Fulfillment of life means joy now and also the building up of the structures needed so that that joy may continue and grow in richness and abundance. The extent to which gambling contributes to or detracts from fulfillment of life is to be judged in terms of the extent to which its admitted thrills have to be bought by the wreckage of future hopes, dreams, and achievements.

The question of illicit sex relations can be decided on the basis of the same basic principles about which we have just been thinking in connection with gambling.

Many other activities also belong here. For example, this quarter includes loss of temper, reckless spending, overeating, oversmoking, overdrinking, and aggressive war.

Every activity in the plus-minus quarter uses energy in wasteful or destructive ways. The word *de-structive* means "tearing down structures." This waste of energies is called also *dissipation*. John Bunyan in his *Pilgrim's Progress* told of an area where such activities are characteristic. He called it "Vanity Fair." It has also sometimes been called "the primrose path." But we may label this quarter with the more obvious words *dissipation* and *vice*.

We have been exploring together the two quarters on the right-hand side of our diagram, where experience is joyous at the start. Let us turn for a moment to the upper left-hand region of the diagram, to

The minus-plus quarter

In this quarter, pain turns to joy. All the experiences that belong here are, at the start, arduous, difficult, painful, toilsome, or at first frustrating. Take, for example, a piece of drudgery that has to be done in order that some creative result may later be achieved. A mother is absorbed in the creative task of bringing up a baby. But in the early stages of that project there are diapers to be changed and to wash or to dispose of. The gardener dreams of the flowers and vegetables that he and God are going to create. But he finds that there is an immense amount of weeding to be done. The salesman dreams of earning a top salary with a rich bonus, but there are countless slow-to-respond and even antagonistic prospects to be approached and persuaded. Drudgery, then, certainly belongs in this quarter.

Then, also up here in this minus-plus quarter belong frugality and thrift. Here is a young man who has been eager to get married. He has a lovely girl who shares his dream of making a home together and rearing a family of children. But this ambitious boy does not want to drag his future wife and his expected children down into poverty. He wants to provide them with a truly beautiful home, and with the resources and the income by means of which they may be able to achieve the abundant life with him. To do that, these lovers face the fact that they have to save some money. For the time being they have to deny themselves many luxuries. Much of their earnings have to go into the savings-and-loan account instead of into the night club. But for the joy that is set before them, they endure the temporary privation.

Another thing that belongs in the minus-plus quarter is chastity—chastity in the best and wisest meaning of that word. A few years ago there was a popular song which went: "I'm saving myself for you!" Young people who dream of future married life together, with loyalty and faithful love, may recognize that during the engagement period a degree of sexual self-discipline and privation may be necessary in order that they may together build up the structures needed for future joy. Here, too, belongs the young man who is engaged or recently married, and who remains faithful to his beloved while absent on military service; here also belongs the wife or sweetheart who does the same thing.

Men and women who toil long hours at difficult and sometimes boring work in order to win high achievement in their careers provide still another example. The man who keeps his temper when he is insulted, the man who endures the pain of a critical operation in order to have his health restored, the mother who is patient with fretful and unreasonable children in order to help them develop character and emotional maturity—all these belong in the minus-plus quarter. Every triumph over temptation belongs here.

The Catholics have a word for a spiritual state after death in which persons who have blundered in their earth life may earn forgiveness and be prepared for life in heaven. Even though the hardships of the minus-plus quarter are not necessarily due to past sins, let us borrow the Catholic word and call this quarter *purgatory*.

The minus-minus quarter is hell on earth

In the lower left-hand corner of the diagram belong all the activities that both cause pain and frustration now and destroy. This is the quarter where activities not only are agonizing, shameful and self-defeating, but where they also tear down the structures needed for future joy. The paroxysms of hate that sometimes accompany the last stages of a marriage breaking up into divorce, the horror and torture of the condemned murderer waiting in the death cell, the anguish of the hopeless drink addict who did not join Alcoholics Anonymous, the devastated life of the gambler who has embezzled money and is being taken to jail, the miseries of Hitler's dictatorship as he brought Germany down into abysmal ruin at the end of World War II—these are but illustrations of what happens to people whose activities have landed them in the minus-minus quarter.

THE FOUR QUARTERS PROVIDE GUIDANCE ABOUT TEMPTATION

Beaten paths lead from Vanity Fair to Hell

Anyone who plunges recklessly into plus-minus activities is risking or even asking for the misery that comes when vital structures of his personality are damaged or shattered through the results of his dissipation and vice.

And from Purgatory to Heaven

Those who endure hardship find, often amazingly soon, that Purgatory provides a gateway to Heaven. It is something like taking a swim on a cool summer morning. We may stand shivering and teetering at the end of the springboard, but when we finally get up the courage to dive in we find that the chill we had feared turns into a tingling joy. The water is wonderful. So, too, young people who save their money, and who maintain loyal devotion to one another before marriage, find that the seeming privation and hardship of this plus-minus period turns into jubilant fulfillment later when they launch forth into married life.

> They climbed the steep ascent of Heaven
> Through peril, toil and pain.
> O God, to us may grace be given
> To follow in their train!

The path of the Prodigal may be charted

The Prodigal Son started in the minus-plus quarter. He was feeding flocks and toiling in his father's fields, bossed around by his older brother. So he demanded his inheritance and cut down across the diagram into the plus-minus quarter, where he wasted his substance in riotous living. Wine, women, and wagering kept him busy for a while. But before long this young Jew found himself in a pigsty. Knowing how Jews feel about swine, wouldn't that be Hell? There he was, down in the depths of the minus-minus quarter.

Then he began to feel guilty. He decided to climb back up the steep, rocky, thorny path that leads through the minus-minus quarter, and to fall at his father's feet saying: "Father, I have sinned against Heaven, and in thy sight: I am no longer worthy to be called thy son: make me as one of thy hired servants." And the path led back thus into the plus-plus quarter.

The four quarters are not arbitrary moral rules

They are not restrictions laid down merely for the purpose of taking the joy out of life. No, the conditions for joyous fulfillment are inherent in the very nature of existence. This is the road to life: stay in the upper two quarters, where every action builds up structures needed for future fulfillment, and you will live abundantly, radiantly, and joyfully. But if your steps or mine wander heedlessly down into the primrose paths of Vanity Fair, if we become so absorbed in getting joy now that we ignore the need to build up the structures required for future joy, then we, like the Prodigal Son, shall find how easy is the descent into the minus-minus quarter, into our own hell on earth.

We need to be delivered from temptation

In the prayer most often prayed in Christendom we have uttered over and over again the words: "Lead us not into temptation, but deliver us from evil." How is this prayer to be made effective in our lives?

Our diagram gives us clear insight into the meaning of temptation. When the impulse, the desire, the longing for joy now, lures us down toward the plus-minus quarter, that is temptation. When we dare to enter into and to spend time and effort in the minus-plus quarter instead of the plus-minus quarter, that is resisting temptation. When we come to ourselves in the minus-minus quarter and begin to aspire to climb back up to the upper half of the diagram, that is repentance. Now then: how can deep prayer empower us to resist temptation, and, if we have failed to resist, how can it help us to repent effectively?

We all want to achieve fulfillment of life. We may all give our intellectual consent to the need to build up structures to that end. But you and I find that we are creatures of impulse. We are bombarded over and over again with temptation. The urge to find joy-now recklessly presents itself quite often in robes of disguise—which makes it look beautiful and even wholesome and creative. Not many of us plunge into Vanity Fair with the intent to do damage to ourselves and others. Most of us have made the very best resolutions that we will refrain from those activities that we have learned to be damaging and destructive. Most of us mean to lead good lives and to follow the ascending road to heaven—on earth and beyond the gates of death. The spirit indeed is willing, but the flesh is weak. We find ourselves in the same impasse as that which was reached by the Apostle Paul when he said: "The good which I would I do not: but the evil which I would not, that I practice."

Since we want to achieve fulfillment of life, we must find some answer to this baffling problem. The good resolutions, which we have made and broken, mock us. There is no way to lift ourselves by our bootstraps. How can we live the kind of lives we really want to live when we see life clearly and see it whole? How can we be the kind of people that we ourselves at our best, with our clearest vision, want to be?

AA'S HAVE DEMONSTRATED SPIRITUAL DELIVERANCE FROM DEADLY TEMPTATION

The possibility of finding a triumphantly successful answer to such questions has been demonstrated by the fact that members of Alcoholics Anonymous have conquered temptation by adventuring spiritually.

Psychiatry had found the problem difficult

Among the most baffling and discouraging problems that any human being can face in his own life is the realization that he has become a chronic alcoholic.

One of the sanest and best-balanced discussions of the alcoholism problem that has yet appeared is the book *How to Live Without Liquor,** by Ralph A. Habas. He says that in the

---

* Habas, Ralph A., *How to Live Without Liquor* (New American Library of World Literature), 1956.

United States alone there are at least 4,000,000 whose drinking has become a serious problem to themselves and to others. On the basis of his figures it would seem probable that one out of ten of the adult population sooner or later becomes a problem drinker. Moreover, this proportion is increasing.

One evening, several years ago, I was having dinner with a psychiatrist who specialized in this problem. I asked him: "Doctor, what proportion of alcoholics have you found it possible really to cure?"

"Well," he said, "of course we take only the more hopeful cases. Among such (according to my own experience) we are able really to cure about 7 per cent."

Adventuring spiritually has far outdistanced merely psychiatric treatment

A few months after my dinner with the psychiatrist, I was having lunch with a man who was in charge of a hostel in which a chapter of Alcoholics Anonymous was giving aid to drink addicts who were struggling to get back on their feet. I asked him the same question: "What proportion of the people who come to you are you able really to cure?"

"Well," he said, "of course we take only the hopeless cases. Of those who are really down in the gutter, and who are ready to throw themselves upon a Higher Power for aid, we can save 85 per cent."

"How about the other 15 per cent?" I asked.

"If they'll come back and try again," he said, "we'll save 85 per cent of them!"

A somewhat more conservative appraisal of the success of the methods used by Alcoholics Anonymous has been given by Dr. Habas. He reports what he calls the conservative estimate —that of those who join the movement, 50 per cent stop drinking at once, and never take another drink. Another 25 per cent recover eventually after a series of backslidings that may stretch over a period of years. The remaining 25 per cent keep slipping off the wagon, though they may return over and over again after their relapses. Dr. Habas points out: "Considering that AA keeps its doors wide open, and makes no attempt to screen psychopathic personalities or individuals who are not emotionally suited to its program, this estimated three-out-of-four ratio of success may be regarded as phenomenal." This is particularly true in view of the 7 per cent of successes among the more hopeful cases, as reported by the psychiatric specialist.

How the movement started, and how it works

In 1945, in Akron, Ohio, an investment broker and a doctor who had both been problem drinkers and who had found deliverance through adventuring spiritually, formed the Alcoholics Anonymous movement. It now has 4,500 branches, all over the world, with a total of more than 100,000 members.

The basic principles of action, of which full-fledged members of Alcoholics Anonymous have all made use, in order to cease to be problem drinkers, are contained in a program of 12 steps. They are as follows:

1. We admitted we were powerless over alcohol, that our lives had become unmanageable.

2. Came to believe that a Power greater than ourselves could restore us to sanity.

3. Made a decision to turn our will and our lives over to the care of God as we understood Him.

4. Made a searching and fearless moral inventory of ourselves.

5. Admitted to God, to ourselves and to another human being the exact nature of our wrongs.

6. Were entirely ready to have God remove all these defects of character.

7. Humbly asked Him to remove our shortcomings.

8. Made a list of all persons we had harmed, and became willing to make amends to them all.

9. Made direct amends to such people wherever possible, except when to do so would injure them or others.

10. Continued to take personal inventory and when we were wrong, promptly admitted it.

11. Sought through prayer and meditation to improve our conscious contact with God as we understood Him, praying only for knowledge of His will for us and the power to carry that out.

12. Having had a spiritual awakening as the result of these steps, we tried to carry this message to alcoholics and practice these principles in all our affairs.

Conquering alcoholic temptation by laying hold of

Superhuman Power

If you will check over the 12 steps followed by members of AA, you will find that at many points they parallel quite closely the steps suggested in listening prayer and deep prayer, as outlined in the earlier chapters of this present book. We have been defining *miracle* as any effect produced on the material, biological, psychological, and sociological levels of personality by power and wisdom from the spiritual level. In this strict sense, the redemptions of personality that have been achieved through Alcoholics Anonymous have been miraculous.

HOW WE CAN GAIN DELIVERANCE BY APPLYING DEEP PRAYER

Deep prayer focuses purposes on activities that build

The *dedication* that is an essential part of true prayer focuses the aspiration of the spiritual adventurer upon those purposes that belong to God. God is the Creator. He is the One Who builds up the structures needed for the fulfillment of human life. Dedication means, therefore, that the one who truly prays makes powerful within his own heart and mind the purposes that will lead him on into creative living.

But what shall we do when desires and cravings pull and

push us powerfully down into the reckless gratifications of the plus-minus quarter? The healthy bodies of normal young people begin, even in their teens, to crave the excitements and the short-run satisfactions of physical love-making. Good food and delicious delicacies keep luring us even when we are overweight. The social customs of drinking and smoking create cravings that may quite easily bring damage to health, and shortening of life. Even so noble a desire as the craving for justice may become an urge to anger and violence. How can prayer help us to triumph over such powerful temptations?

Condition your unconscious to react creatively

We need to grasp a bit of basic psychology here. Everything that stirs up energy in you is a *stimulus*. The way in which you direct that energy, or the ways in which it explodes without your directing it, are what is meant by your *reaction*. When you yield to temptation you have given a wasteful or destructive reaction to a stimulus. When you resist temptation, and turn the energy into wholesome activities, you have given a constructive reaction.

Psychologists have discovered that it is possible to *condition* your response to a given stimulus. That is to say, you can se-elect in advance the kind of response that you, at your best, really want to give to a given stimulus. Then, by the right use of psychological methods, you can set both your conscious and your unconscious mind so that that wholesome reaction will be the one that leaps out immediately, and even before you can think about it, when that stimulus comes to you.

Deep prayer brings spiritual reinforcement

When you center your attention wholeheartedly and single-mindedly upon the problem, you can give instructions to your own unconscious mind that will result in conditioning yourself so that the desired response will take the place of the wasteful or destructive reaction that previously you have been giving. This method has proved to be powerfully effective, even when used without the aid of religion. But when we take the method over into deep prayer, a still more powerful result may be obtained.

Take some single, simple reaction like overeating, or like losing your temper. By auto-post-hypnotic suggestion you can condition yourself so that when the tempting stimulus comes along you will react to it constructively instead of yielding. Suppose, for example, that the temptation is to lose your temper. The stimulus, let us say, is a very irritating, overbearing associate. When you are deeply relaxed you can say to yourself, "Whenever that person seems to be irritating, that will remind me of all his *good* characteristics. It will make me understanding and friendly." The result of that sort of conditioning can be a very marked improvement in social relationships.

But when this becomes part of true religion, the whole process takes on far deeper significance and power. The dedication and the devotion of the spiritual life reinforce the auto-suggestion. The struggle for mastery is empowered by the Spirit of God. In the profound relaxation, and the serene concentration of deep prayer, the victory over temptation comes with the petition:

> **O, God, under Thy guidance and by Thy power, I will go forward with courage, with character, and with creative love.**

Training yourself to stay away from temptation

The best time to hold back from rash and disastrous acts is before we get too close to the brink. For example, the girl who sincerely wants to avoid getting into sexual difficulties needs to hold without exception to such rules as never to accept invitations from strange men, and never to park with unloved acquaintances, in places where things are likely to occur that the girl will later regret.

Similarly, a boy who wants to avoid letting his sex drive run away with him must school himself not to take the early steps that lead him into situations where temptation becomes overwhelming.

The same principle applies to business honesty. A man who is sincerely loyal to the ideal of carrying out the Golden Rule in all his business relationships will be alert to avoid taking such early steps as accepting a job where he realizes that unethical acts will be expected of him, or entering into agreements that would make him a party to possibly unscrupulous acts by other people.

Usually, if we betray our ideals in any way, that betrayal is the end-result of a series of steps. When we take the first step or two we may quite often be unconscious of the sinister outcome. But form the habit of using deep prayer at the very first moment when you begin to feel uneasy about the moves that you have been making. In deep relaxation, pray this prayer:

> **O God, at the moment when I begin to realize that I am betraying Thee, let that be the signal to me to turn my back on the temptation, and to turn my energy, reinforced by Thy power, into the path of truth, justice, and honor.**

That form of deep prayer is quite in harmony with modern psychology. But it is not too different from what Jesus said. You will remember the account of how he was led up of the Spirit into the wilderness to be tempted of the Devil. After a series of temptations the Devil said to him: "All these things will I give thee, if thou wilt fall down and worship me."

But Jesus said to him:

> Get thee hence, Satan: for it is written, "Thou shalt worship the Lord thy God, and Him only shalt thou serve!"

CONQUERING TEMPTATION MAY BE
SUMMED UP AS FOLLOWS:

Temptation and the plus-plus-minus-minus diagram

At the right-hand end of the horizontal is the plus of "joy now"; at the left end is the minus of "pain and frustration now." At the top of the vertical is the plus of "building up" structures needed for future joy; at the bottom is the minus of "tearing down" such structures. The upper right-hand, the plus-plus quarter, thus contains activities that involve joy now and that build up; the plus-minus quarter at the lower right contains activities that give thrills at the time but that damage structures; the minus-plus quarter on the upper left contains hardships and privations that build up; the minus-minus quarter at the lower left is the hell-on-earth of present misery combined with continuing destruction. Temptation is the lure of the plus-minus quarter; resistance is undertaking the necessity of the minus-plus quarter. Repentance is turning from the lower, minus half up into the minus-plus and then the plus-plus quarter.

Members of AA have adventured spiritually

Whereas a psychiatrist estimated 7 per cent of cures among hopeful cases, the AA movement has been curing 75 per cent of drunkards who had believed their own cases to be hopeless. The 12 steps which members of this movement take involve conquering temptation by laying hold of superhuman power.

Deep prayer gives deliverance from temptation

You can condition your own unconscious to react creatively when temptation stimulates. Deep prayer adds God's power to autoconditioning. And we can train ourselves to stay away from temptation.

Chapter *10*

How to Win a Clean
Conscience by Prayer

WHAT KIND OF CONSCIENCE HAVE YOU?

Everyone who is normal has a conscience. If a person feels no sense of guilt when he has tortured a little child, stolen money from a blind cripple, or told hideous lies about an innocent man or woman, that person may well be called a moral imbecile. You are no moral imbecile, or you would not be reading this book. So what kind of a conscience do *you* have?

Those in charge of young children build their consciences

If your mother was the one who had charge of you most of the time when you were a little child, she was the chief builder of your conscience. When you did some kinds of things she smiled at you, approved of you, rewarded you with praise and with other enjoyments. But when you did things of which your mother disapproved, perhaps she frowned at you; perhaps she spoke to you sharply, or even punished you more or less severely. You have forgotten almost all those experiences, but

131

your unconscious mind has not forgotten. Down in the depths of your personality the effects of those approvals and disapprovals, those rewards and punishments that you received when you were a very small child, are still giving you satisfaction or pain, according to whether you are doing what your deep-down mind thinks is right or that mind thinks is wrong.

Of course, the approvals and disapprovals of other people are likely to give you satisfactions or pains. Indeed, most of us find it very difficult to feel virtuous if those who are dear to us condemn what we are doing. And most of us, most of the time, find it rather easy to go along with the crowd and do the things that lead other people to give us friendly smiles, encouragement, and approval.

Who should feel guilty?

Let us take a look at two cases:

1. A man and his wife had driven to a distant city to attend a convention, leaving their children in the care of the wife's mother. On the evening of the third day of the convention, they received a telegram saying that one of the children was dangerously ill. The man was worn out from conference sessions that had lasted through each of the three days and far into the first two nights. But he felt that he had to drive his wife back home so that she could care for the sick child. They got into their car, and he drove for eight hours steadily, against innumerable blinding lights and over pavements that were often slippery with freezing rain. Then at four o'clock the next morning, after he had been driving for an hour down a straight highway, he dropped asleep at the wheel, and crashed into a telephone pole. When he came back to consciousness, he found that his wife had been killed.

He felt an overwhelming sense of guilt. For years thereafter he hardly even smiled. His four children were afraid of him, and their fear made him feel still more guilty. But should he have felt guilty? He had made a tragic mistake, but he had been doing the very best thing that he knew how to do, and he had been putting forth the utmost of his resources in trying to care for his family. Moreover, the way his guilt feelings worked out meant that he had not only been the unwilling cause of depriving his children of their mother, but he had then compounded the blunder by depriving them of the love and encouragement which he, as their father, should have given them.

2. A six-story factory was being built in a Midwestern city. The basic structure of the building was reinforced concrete. The contractor whose bid had been accepted for the work had been making money rapidly, and was eager to make it still faster. He cut down on the amount of cement called for by the specifications, and (against the urging of his construction foreman) insisted on pouring the concrete for the top story before the lower stories had been sufficiently seasoned. As a result, the entire structure came crashing down, killing six workmen and injuring fifteen others. But this contractor refused to feel guilty. "Accidents will happen!" he asserted. "Those specifications were completely unreasonable. Anyhow it was the foreman's fault!"

In this case not only should the contractor have felt guilty, but community indignation was justified in seeking to drive home to him and to all contractors the realization that such reckless breaking of the law and risking of human lives cannot be tolerated. Actually, the contractor was indicted, and served a term in prison.

Some basic rules about guilt

Our conclusions from cases like the two cited above can be summed up in a brief series of simple rules:

1. Feelings of guilt are valuable when they help us to learn from past mistakes and sins, so as to hold us back from future actions that would damage ourselves and other people.

2. No one should feel guilty merely because he was involved

in some damaging or even disastrous event, provided that no reasonable effort on his part would have prevented the damage.

3. Most of us need to learn to shoulder bravely whatever guilt is really ours, and to learn from such painful experiences how to avoid future wrongdoing.

4. Most of us need help from sources beyond ourselves, and from sources higher than human, in order to be freed from poisonous and destructive forms of guilt feelings.

THE WOMAN WHO FELT GUILTY ABOUT LOVE WITH HER HUSBAND

Some years ago I was delivering a series of addresses at a winter retreat held in a suburb of one of our great cities. At the close of an address in which the power of prayer was described, a woman (whom we will call Mrs. X) asked for a private interview. When we were alone she asked me: "Do you think prayer can save me from my sense of guilt?"

I asked her to tell me why she felt guilty. She said that she had been married for eight years. She and her husband had two children. She had only recently been discharged from her third stay in a psychiatric hospital. She said she had had this series of nervous breakdowns because of an overwhelming sense of guilt.

When I asked her why she felt guilty, she said that before she married her husband she had been deeply in love with another man. She realized that the man she loved would never make a reliable husband. He had an artistic temperament. He had never held a steady job. He had no sense of the value of money. He was apt to have flights of rapturous enthusiasm, followed by periods of dark depression. And yet she loved him with all her heart—overwhelmingly and consumingly.

While she was struggling with the problem of what to do about this love, another man began courting her. This man was steady, reliable, and devoted. He had been working at one place for five years, and had been promoted several times. He told her that she was the one woman in the world for him and that he would do everything in his power to make her happy.

When she told him that she did not really love him he said: "Give me a chance. I'll make you love me!" So finally, out of heartrending conflict, she yielded and married her present husband. Her husband had kept his word completely, and had been utterly faithful and loving. He had brought home his pay regularly and adequately; he had provided a good home and a good living for her and the children. But every time she had sex relations with him, she kept feeling the terrible surge of her love for the man she had given up. This experience convinced her that she was committing adultery when she was in bed with her husband. Since she was a deeply religious woman, this mental conflict had brought on a series of breakdowns that had led to her repeated commitment to the hospital.

After she had explained the situation to me, she asked me what to do. I told her to relax deeply in the comfortable chair in which she was sitting, resting her head back against the upholstery. She closed her eyes, and after a few suggestions of letting go she said that she was feeling deeply relaxed and at peace. Then I said to her:

"It is right for you to have loved this other man. Your heart can still hold his memory with affection and gratitude. But now it would be a sin not to give yourself freely and with utter love to the man you have married.

"I want you to visualize the loving Christ, standing here beside you. The loving Christ says to you:

> You have promised in my name, to love, honor and cherish this your husband. It is my will that you fulfill that vow with all your heart. Give yourself to him lovingly, joyously, and in my spirit. This is the utterly holy and Christian thing to do. Hereafter you will do this with joy, and with deep peace in your heart."

The next day this woman came back, utterly radiant. She said that she had had a supreme spiritual experience. Her heart and her mind were filled with love and joy. She asked me whether she might drive back to the city and bring her husband out to talk with me. He had been staying home with the children while she was attending the retreat. When he came, he seemed a little bewildered, but relieved and happy that she had found joy.

Year after year since then I have heard from this family. This woman has been leading a healthy-minded, useful, and often joyous life. She became an outstanding leader in the work of her church. The power of her spiritual life became contagious, inspiring her friends, bringing about activities that quickened the spiritual life of her community.

FORGIVENESS HEALS

Are you carrying a load of guilt?

In Bunyan's *Pilgrim's Progress*, Pilgrim is pictured as one who dwelt in the City of Destruction, and who carried about, strapped to his shoulders, a heavy load of guilt. Actually, a rather large proportion of all those who tread the streets of any city, or the paths of any farm, carry such a load—not physically on their backs, but deep in their minds. Most of the time these guilt feelings may be pushed back into the unconscious, but many people wake up in the night, when they should be sleeping, and toss in anguish because of the recollection of blunders which they have made, of pain which they have inflicted on loved ones or on working associates, and of failures in which they have fallen far short of the high dreams, hopes, and ideals that they have cherished. Quite often those who have been damaged by the sleepless person's sins are long since dead, or far beyond the reach of any restitution that the guilty one can make. Indeed, this may make the feelings of guilt still more poignant. Quite often the guilty pangs thus suffered merely wear down the energy and the courage of the guilty one, and bring no hopeful or creative result.

Confess your sins

Confession is so vital a step in seeking freedom from guilt that the Catholic Church has made it one of its basic sacraments. To hear confession is one of the major duties of the priest. But this is by no means exclusively a Catholic practice. Much of the help that troubled people get from consulting psychoanalysts and other types of psychotherapists and counselors is the opportunity to unburden the soul by confession.

When Frank Buchman founded the Moral Rearmament Movement, one of its most sensational features was the public confessions that were held at the house parties set up by the Buchmanites. Some of these were so sensational that damage was done, and criticism was aroused. But the powerful effect of unburdening the soul by confession was one of the major factors that contributed to the growth and the effectiveness of the Moral Rearmament Movement.

If it is granted that confession is often a powerful source of relief, and a step toward healthy-minded living, and granting also the fact that it has its dangers, what basic rules can we accept? Let's start with these:

1. When you have wronged someone, and when your relations with that person can be straightened out and made wholesome once again by owning up to the wrong and offering to do your best to make amends, then confess *to that person* in such a way as to heal the damage and restore friendly cooperative relationships.

2. Do not confess simply to relieve your own mind, when the confession is likely to do more harm than good.

3. Take care not to use the confession as a form of exhibitionism—a way of attracting attention and trying to get other people to admire your sanctity.

4. Seek spiritual guidance as to when and how confession

can be made so as to restore good will and to build up creative and wholesome activities.

5. In a word, think of confession as a painful but potentially powerful aid toward cleansing guilt and rebuilding good will.

Go and be reconciled

That is not only a divine command; it is the sane and sensible next step toward relieving the poisonous pressure. But reconciliation calls for a preliminary step.

Make restitution

If you have any guilty feelings from which you long to be purged, ask yourself first this question: "What can I do to right the wrong that makes me thus feel guilty?" Confession is no substitute for the righting of wrongs—so far as such righting lies within our power. Sometimes it will be costly and painful to make restitution, but the cost and the pain must be accepted courageously and honestly if we are to be freed from guilt. Sometimes the damage which has been done is beyond repair. It may help in such cases to seek some way in which we can perform some creative act to help counterbalance the damage we have done. If our sins and blunders have caused sorrow, let that be a stimulus to seek out some way in which we can give joy, either to those who have suffered from our wrongdoing or (if that is not possible) to someone else.

When you ask the question: "What can I do to right the wrong?" the answer may not, at first, be crystal clear. In that case, use listening prayer to get more light upon it. Search deeply, honestly, and courageously to find out how, even at deep cost to yourself, you can right the wrong that you have done. This is a first and basic step toward freedom from guilt.

Ask for earthly forgiveness

When we seek reconciliation, part of the penance is to humble ourselves, to reach out suppliant hands, seeking restoration of good will and of friendly cooperation. To make such a plea may seem costly in terms of pride, but it can be deeply rewarding in renewal of fellowship and in freeing the heart from self-condemnation.

Seek divine forgiveness

To ask forgiveness of those whom we have wronged is a first step that must be taken whenever it is possible and right to do so. But when we have cleared away the roots of guilt so far as that can be done by seeking human forgiveness, we may still have, burdening our hearts, the load of wrongs that cannot be righted. Let us remember, then, that God is infinitely forgiving. When we have done our best to heal the wounds caused by our own wrong actions, the love of God can cleanse and cure the remaining wounds.

**For the love of God is broader than the measure of
man's mind,
And the heart of the Eternal is most wonderfully kind.**

Be forgiving

How often we have prayed: "Forgive us our trespasses as we forgive those who trespass against us." We seek to be part of the kind of a world in which resentment, reprisals, and antagonisms will no longer exist. To get other people to give up socially destructive attitudes is often beyond our power. But one thing does lie within our control—namely, to cleanse our own hearts and lives of such attitudes. That is an achievement readily within our power if we make full use of deep prayer.

To understand is to forgive

To say: "I forgive you," may have a sort of "I'm holier than you are" flavor about it. The one who thus gives forgiveness may be feeling, more or less unconsciously, that he is proving his superiority to the one who is being forgiven. That kind of moral strutting does little good; indeed it may merely create new tensions and antagonisms.

Try the triangle of brotherly prayer in seeking to establish a better relationship with the one who seems to need your forgiveness. Think of the love of God flowing around him, and then wait and listen receptively for illumination that may show you why this person acted in the way that hurt and offended you. Everything that anyone does springs from some sort of reasons and causes. If we put ourselves in the other person's place, if we think how we might have acted if we had been under similar pressures and temptations, then we may find that really there is nothing to forgive.

Actually, what we need is not any merely condescending surrender of what may have been our craving for vengeance. Rather what we should seek is mutual understanding, a readiness to turn our backs on past blunders after we have learned our lessons from them, and a spirit of cooperative friendliness so that in the future we may work together for the common good.

Forgive yourself

Let us suppose that you have blundered and sinned. You yourself have come to realize it. You feel a deep sense of guilt. Perhaps you even have come to despise or to hate yourself at times. If so, that means that you need to use deep prayer. You need to learn to forgive—not only your enemies but also yourself. Remember that guilt feelings are justified only in so far as they make you better and wiser in the future. Never go on punishing yourself when that punishment is making you less fit to be a member of the Beloved Community. Forgive yourself. Seek God's forgiveness, and the forgiveness of anyone whom you may have damaged. And then go forward with courage, with faith, and with joy.

LEARN TO LIVE GUILTLESSLY

Feelings of guilt have a vital part to play in helping to restrain us from evil and damaging activities, as long as we need that kind of restraint. But only the emotionally and spiritually immature do actually need to be controlled by guilt feelings. He who day by day practices listening prayer and deep prayer can learn creatively to avoid and refrain from the wrong actions and the blunders that would call later for feelings of guilt. Learn not to walk in the path of temptation. Learn to refrain from yielding when unavoidable temptation comes. The results will be far better than having to cleanse away the damages and the guilt that surge in after one has yielded.

But those things are negative. What we need most is to learn to live positively. Learn to live lovingly and creatively. Practice the three Do's systematically. Learn to live the life of the spirit. As the Apostle Paul put it:

> The harvest of the spirit is love, joy, peace, good temper, kindliness, generosity, fidelity, gentleness, self-control:—there is no law against those who practice such things. . . . As we live by the Spirit, let us be guided by the Spirit; let us have no vanity, no provoking, no envy of one another. Even if anyone is detected in some trespass, brothers, you are spiritual, you must set the offender right in the spirit of gentleness; let each of you look to himself in case he too is tempted. Bear one another's burdens. . . .

If we live in that spirit, problems of guilt will fade out of our lives.

HOW TO BE PURGED FROM GUILT CAN BE SUMMED UP THUS

We need to take our full share of blame when we deserve it. But most of us need help from sources higher than human in order to be freed from poisonous guilt feelings.

Forgiveness heals. Confess—when that will truly help. Be reconciled; make restitution; ask forgiveness; be forgiving. Forgive yourself.

Learning to live guiltlessly is better than having to cleanse away the damages and the remorse that spring from yielding to temptation.

‡‡‡

Chapter 11

Prayer Can Transform Lives

"We know that we have passed out of death into life."

That is the way one of the early Christians expressed the magnitude of the transformation that had come to him because he had entered into the great spiritual adventure.

But just what is the nature of the transformation that has come to the spiritual adventurer in the quest that we have been following together up to this point? Let us set down the contrast, point by point:

> He has found God. The spiritual seeker has discovered that he lives, and moves, and has his being in a supreme, creative Intelligence, whose goals are love, beauty, truth and joy. This is not a blind universe— it is not a heartless machine. It is the work of God, and the spiritual seeker can become a co-creator with the superhuman intelligence and power by which he himself was created.
>
> The spiritual adventurer no longer dreads death. Instead of cruel severance of loving relations, he has become aware of ongoing communion. Instead of blank extinction at the end of earthly life, he has found reason to look forward to magnificent continu-

ance of the spiritual adventure beyond death's gate-way.

He has found the road to fulfillment of life. That is the goal of religion. Devotion to great projects is the secret. He has learned to be guided out of his per-plexities by means of listening prayer. And he has learned to banish discouragement, loneliness, guilt, antagonism—and the other emotions of depression and failure by means of deep prayer.

"While I breathe I pray!"

One of the great hymns of the church puts this victory into dramatic form. It represents the Tempter as trying to bring doubt, discouragement, and misery into the heart of the Chris-tian. The hymn goes on:

> Christian, answer boldly,
> While I breathe, I pray;
> Peace shall follow battle;
> Night shall end in day.

How deep and far-reaching the transformation can be stands out more clearly if we think about it for a few moments in terms of the story of Tom and Anne.

THE LIVES OF LOVERS CAN BE TRANSFORMED BY LOVE

Finding your true love transforms life

Tom was a boy from a small town who had graduated from school and then taken a job in a big city. He lived in a fur-nished room. When he first rented it he thought that it was very nice and comfortable. He looked forward to going to his room after his work was over and doing some reading. But it wasn't many days until Tom began to find that same room terribly lonely. Five nights a week Tom would go to the movies, just to get away from that place that now seemed so empty and so forlorn.

Anne had grown up on a farm. She too had graduated and taken a job in the city. She too had found a furnished room. She fixed it up with fluffy curtains, and she got her breakfast and her supper in the little kitchenette, pretending all the while that she was keeping house, practicing up for that wonder boy for whom she hoped some time she might be making a home. But her room also got to be almost unbearably lonely. Just to get away from it, she would go out in the park and talk to the birds.

One Sunday she was talking back to the mourning dove: "That noise you're making is just the way I feel!" She almost jumped out of her shoes when she heard a boy's voice replying: "And that's just the way I feel too!" It was Tom. He happened to be sitting on the bench just back of hers, and when he heard the mourning dove and heard Anne speak he couldn't stop himself from joining in.

That was the start of a new dawn for both of them. Suddenly, instead of dreading the hour when they would have to go back to their lonely rooms, they began to look forward eagerly to the moment when they would be together and go on sharing each other's lives. Within six months they were married and were trying to make the grass grow around a new little cottage out in the suburbs.

It was a shining new life for both of them. The first year was marvelous. There were troubles, but they took them together, as a gallant team. Then, gradually, the shine wore off.

A deeper transformation is needed

Tom failed to get promoted. Then he quit his job and was out of work for two months. Black disaster came when their baby toddled out into the street and was killed by a passing car.

To Anne, the anguish seemed almost unbearable. In desperation, one late afternoon, she stopped in at a church where she saw a door ajar. It "happened" that there was a little group of people there who were experimenting together with the power of "prayer therapy." They welcomed Anne. She took a seat, although at first she felt doubt and distrust. But before a half hour had passed, a warmth had begun to enfold her heart. A new light began to shine. She found comfort and new vision. She hurried home to tell Tom about it. Reluctantly, and in dull unbelief, he agreed to go with her to the next meeting of the "prayer therapy" group. Then he too experienced the power.

Their bitterness faded away. They found courage to go forward, and within a year their hearts were comforted by a new baby. Their early dreams of joy together found new and richer fulfillment.

MAN'S EXTREMITY CAN BE GOD'S OPPORTUNITY

The transformation that Anne and Tom experienced came as a result of using systematic prayer therapy. But quite often lives are transformed by a much less methodical outreach toward God. That fact is illustrated by the following experience:

Out of despair, she found God

Some years ago I was delivering in Washington, D.C. a series of lectures, held under the auspices of the Council of Churches. At the close of the second lecture in that series, a cluster of people had come up to ask questions and to make comments. As I was talking with one of these, a woman stepped quickly toward me, thrust an envelope into my hands, said: "Read it when you get a chance!" and then scurried away. I shoved it absentmindedly into my pocket and went on with my conversation. When I got home that night, I found the envelope, and I discovered that it contained an unsigned letter. In it the woman said that, since I had been talking about making contact with spiritual power, she thought I might be interested in an experience that had come to her four years previously.

She said that the experience had come at a time when she felt that her life had collapsed in complete disaster. She felt that she had wrecked her life; that she was no longer worthy of respect from her acquaintances nor of the love of her husband. She was sitting in her home, in the inward darkness of despair. The sink was piled high with dirty dishes; the beds were not made; the furniture had not been dusted, and soiled clothing lay scattered on the floor.

She said that she had not been reading the Bible or any religious literature. She had simply been overwhelmed with bleak disheartenment and self-disgust. Suddenly, out of her despair, she heard herself cry: "O God, help me!" Instantly an experience swept over her that she had never had before, and which she said that she had not had again since that day. She felt her whole being flooded with the utter, radiant joy of God. She knew, beyond any doubt, that the love, the beauty, and the goodness of God pervade the entire universe. She knew that this love and this radiant power were enfolding her, bearing her up, clearing away the murk that had been darkening her soul. She was filled with divine ecstasy.

She wrote in her letter that she did not know how long this experience lasted. Gradually the radiant bliss died down. Then she said: "You may think this odd, but what I did was to get up, go to the telephone, and order that some groceries be sent out to the house." Then she went to the sink and began washing the dirty dishes. In a little while a delivery boy came to the door. When he saw her face he stared at her open-eyed and open-mouthed. "My, but you look happy!" he exclaimed. A little later her husband came home. He had been expecting to find her still overwhelmed with misery. But to his joyful surprise he found her deeply and profoundly transformed.

That transformation had lasted. Though the glory never came back in full tide, it had basically changed her life.

Men as well as women have been saved from the brink

The annals of Alcoholics Anonymous contain thousands of such cases. Men who have come to realize that they are obsessed with the gambling impulse, men who have found themselves brought to the brink of utter defeat by their own undisciplined sex impulses, men who have faced failure and ruin in their business or in their professional lives—these are examples of the fact that men as well as women have found power and wisdom, from above and beyond themselves, when they have reached out for it in their times of desperate need.

LAYING HOLD OF THE POWER

Ask yourself this question: Do you believe that there is in the universe a Wisdom above all human wisdom, and a Power above all human power?

If your answer to that first question is yes, then ask yourself this second one: Do you believe that this Superhuman Power and Wisdom have been at work, in ages past, through the Hebrew prophets and through Jesus of Nazareth and his disciples, to transform human personalities and through them to transform the world?

If you do, we come then to the really crucial question: Do you believe that that Power and that Wisdom are just as much available to you and to me now, today, as they ever have been to anyone anywhere in ages past?

If you, in response to this third question, answer yes, you confront yourself with one of the most basic challenges of life. The challenge is this: Since we believe in the vital significance of this reality, we must each one of us ask ourselves: "Why am I not more fully in touch with this Wisdom and this Power? How can I learn to have it flow more fully and more gloriously through my daily life, into my daily actions, and out into rich and creative achievements?"

Contact through deep prayer

If we aspire to become initiates into spiritual truth, our supreme responsibility is to learn to hear and to respond to spiritual guidance. Somewhere in the lower back part of the brain of every one of us there appears to be located some sort of spiritual receiving set. We can, if we will, tune in to the faint signals that come to us from those who are ready to be our spiritual guides and inspirers. By the aid of deep prayer we can tune out the static of our worries and anxieties. We can obtain divine aid in eliminating the interference of our passions, our greeds, and our fears. By means of courage and faith we can climb the steep ascent of heaven with vision, and with joy.

SOME CHANGES THAT SHINE OUT IN TRANSFORMED LIVES

The new grip on life that Anne and Tom found through the prayer group, and that came to the woman in Washington in response to her despairing cry for divine help, can be achieved by every seeker who learns to use deep prayer. To those who thus establish full working relations with Superhuman Power, there comes a profound transformation of life. Here are some of the basic changes that life undergoes when listening prayer and deep prayer take full effect.

He leadeth me

Most of us hunger for security. We live in a world of peril. The job through which you earn your living, the little son or daughter to whom you have given your heart in utter love, the husband or wife whom you have trusted—such treasures are infinitely precious. Any menace to them menaces us. But he who has found the true meaning of prayer has made a great discovery: "I only know I cannot drift beyond His love and care." The Good Shepherd leads you. You can trust him utterly. For you, all things can work together for good, because your life can be united with this transforming power.

That joy may be made full

Every great project has difficulties, hardships, and dangers. We have seen that fact in some detail in earlier chapters. But he who has been transformed spiritually knows that the fundamental pattern of creative life is joyous. The sources of misery have been effectually and lastingly abolished from the transformed life. Death holds no menace; resentment and antagonism are gone; fear is permanently eliminated; fundamental defeat is impossible.

These deliverances clear the way for joy. But when your life is spiritually transformed you will not be content merely to have turned your back on gloom and discouragement. In your daily period of prayer you will commit yourself to the pattern of basically joyous living. You are called to live a life that shines with joy. Even when pain, suffering, and sorrow are part of the harvest of your life projects, you will remember the ancient promise: "Your sorrow will be changed into joy."

The miasma of hatred gives way to good will

Universal love may seem at first to be a far-off and an impossible dream. But let us suppose that you could be fully and unquestioningly confident that *no one* can really damage you so long as you walk in the love of God. Suppose that you have learned to use the triangle of brotherly prayer, and have found that its miracle-working power is available in *every* case and on *every* occasion when hate and resentment might otherwise poison a relationship. Suppose that you have discovered through actual practice that to understand *is* to forgive.

Let there be no misunderstanding here. The attitude of creative universal love is not a sentimental appeasement of evil. It is not a rosy-spectacled distortion of injustice and exploitation into pretended satisfaction. Rather, the spiritual discovery is that when we carry out the Three Do's, when we always change menace to promise by courage, when we always find comrade and partner creators, and when we always adventure with guidance transcendent, making continuing use of listening prayer and deep prayer, then there is no evil in the world that can bring to us disaster and defeat. "Thanks be to God Who giveth us the victory"—not the victory of crushing and destroying others, but the victory of constructive love, and of patient, friendly labor toward bringing the divine dream into realization.

Truth is Reality Incarnate

The transformed life builds on deep reverence for truth. Since God is real, Reality is God. The truth is Reality in humanly understandable terms. The scientist, in so far as he is utterly loyal to the truth, is a priest and prophet of the Divine. We shall know the truth, and the truth will make us free.

There is no death

"Out, out brief candle!" was the despairing cry of Macbeth. Those who have wrecked their own lives, and who have failed to find the spiritual answer to their problems, may share Macbeth's feeling that "tomorrow, and tomorrow and tomorrow creeps in this petty pace from day to day." To such people death may come to seem like a ruined doorway leading out into utter darkness. But the spiritually transformed learn to live in the shining faith of ongoing life, and of love that conquers death.

You have magnificent work to do

Those who have not yet found the spiritual answer may feel condemned to the dreary treadmill of distasteful toil, or may suffer still more poignant bitterness of being discarded as useless and unwanted. But those who live in the light find challenging undertakings always calling for their aspiration and their creative effort. The task lies before us. The challenge quickens us. As one hymn-writer put it:

> Awake, my soul, stretch ev'ry nerve,
> And press with vigor on;
> A heav'nly race demands thy zeal,
> And an immortal crown.

This day our daily bread

Economic security looms up for many as toweringly important. This can be outstandingly true if you have been unemployed, or if your family budget seems hopelessly out of balance, or if you have suffered financial disaster. But that familiar phrase in the Lord's Prayer—"Give us this day our daily bread" —embodies a trust and faith that the transformed life finds to be deeply reliable. Whatever material necessities may be needed to carry on our spiritual enterprise will be provided us, if we are wholeheartedly and unreservedly dedicated to the spiritual quest.

"Let us run with patience the race that is set before us"

The spiritually awakened man knows that he has a strenuous course to run. Like the athlete in the Coliseum "with all this host of witnesses encircling us, we must strip off every handicap, strip off sin with its clinging folds, to run our appointed course steadily." To have awakened spiritually means that you have accepted a tremendous challenge. You have committed yourself under the gaze of your fellow men. Having committed ourselves, let us go forward with unflagging energy.

TRANSFORMED LIVES ARE UNITED
IN FELLOWSHIP

The transformed life has been delivered forever from an isolated loneliness. The very essence of this spiritual transformation consists in entering into a fellowship based on universal love. Accept as your goal fulfillment of life for all men. By that very act you enter into partnership with every other person who makes that dedication. The doors of fellowship stand wide open in your heart. Your comrades, with their hearts wide open to fellowship, are all about you. You are bound to find them, for love is the power that unites. There is no enslavement in this fellowship; where the spirit of love is, there is liberty.

You must be born again

That is what the Great Teacher said to Nicodemus, who came at night to question him. To be freed from fear, discouragement, guilt, hatred, and resentment, to discover that brotherly love and creative achievement can be the keynotes of our lives—these realizations can be an actual rebirth out of darkness and depression into light and joy.

THE TRANSFORMATION CAN BE SUMMED UP THUS

We know that we have passed out of death into life. The spiritual adventurer has found God. He no longer dreads death. He has found the road to fulfillment of life through listening prayer and deep prayer.

Each of us experiences a somewhat similar transformation when we find our true life partner, and set forth in joyous and creative life together. But a deeper transformation is needed. We need to establish working relations with Superhuman Power and Wisdom. This can be achieved through listening prayer and deep prayer.

In everyone whose life and personality have been transformed by this superhuman contact, the following changes shine out:

He has discovered that he can trust himself utterly to the Power above all human power.

He knows that the fundamental pattern of creative life is joyous.

The miasma of hatred has given way to good will.

The transformed life is built on deep reverence for the truth.

Shining faith in ongoing life has conquered death.

Challenging undertakings keep calling for creative efforts.

He knows that whatever material necessities may be needed to carry on the spiritual enterprise will be provided.

He runs with patience the race that is set before him.

His life is united in fellowship with other transformed lives.

Book **III**

How You Can Put Religion
Into Daily Living

Chapter 12

Love and Courage
Can Remake Marriage

We have been thinking together about how prayer can transform lives. Listening prayer can illuminate the paths whereby the seeker can climb out of the bogs of depression and antagonism, and can find the road to courage, to friendly good will and achievement. Deep prayer can give the seeker the power to put the vision into action.

Heaven begins at home

When we cherish dreams about happiness we need to remember one thing: only the deed can bring the reward. You and I believe truly that joyous and creative comradeship *can* be achieved if we rightly use listening prayer and deep prayer. But the reward of this knowledge will come to us only to the extent that we carry out the steps with full devotion and with continuing persistence.

The ideal social order based on brotherly love is referred to in the New Testament as "the Kingdom of God." Even more truly, this ideal social order is the *Family* of God, based on divine Fatherhood and human brotherhood. For us individually, the place to start the Family of God is in our own homes.

Some practical working rules

The test of our devotion to these ideals, and the measure of our success in attaining them, are to be found in the degree to which we achieve creative and joyous cooperation in our face-to-face relationships. Once we are committed to this ideal, the problem becomes one of using our full intelligence to make effective that to which we aspire and to make it effective day by day and hour by hour. Here in this chapter are presented, in down-to-earth terms, some working rules that have proved to be practically useful in transforming family life more and more into an effective unit of the Beloved Community.

"COME WHAT MAY, I WILL SEEK THY JOY!"

Religious marriage ceremonies almost always contain a promise. This promise is at the very heart of the marriage vows. Both the bride and the groom promise "to love and to cherish till death do us part."

But how can you promise lifelong love? Love is a profound emotion that seems to spring up out of the roots of our being. When it first comes, it is likely to seem to be a rapturous gift from God Himself, something that is like the sunrise, or like the dawn of spring. But when love departs, it often also seems a loss quite beyond the intention or the purpose of the husband and wife who once were so deeply devoted to one another. How can a verbal promise, no matter how solemnly the vow is made, take control over these deep surges of the human spirit?

Yet there is a promise that the bride and the groom *can* make, a promise over whose fulfillment they *can* have deliberate and purposeful control. The promise is this: "Come what may, I will seek thy joy!" To seek the joy of your life partner is a deliberate action, and the sane and emotionally mature person can control such actions. Put into other words, this promise means: "In whatever I do relating to you, I will seek so to act as to help to bring to you the greatest fulfillment of life." That is an action pattern, something to be cultivated deliberately, and carried out purposefully during the whole course of your marriage.

This promise, however, is a very broad and sweeping one. It is something like saying: "I am going to get a college education!" Or, it is like saying: "I am taking a new job, and I hereby resolve to work at that job so faithfully, so industriously, and so intelligently that I will reach the highest level of success." Any such broad promise has to be worked out detail by detail, day after day, month after month, and year after year.

Some of the concrete meaning of the promise to seek fulfillment of joy for your life partner may be conveyed by thinking in terms of actual cases. Here are two illustrations that may well lead off our thinking about the meaning of married love.

She longed to have a baby

Isabelle Jones was married to a high school principal in a medium-sized city. He was 27 years old at the time they were married; she was 22. This was a first marriage for both of them.

Her husband, Edgar, was wonderfully kind to her. He was always gentle and considerate. He took her in as full partner in relation to the family finances. He took an active interest in the furnishing of their home and the beautification of the garden around their house. He brought her little gifts, and took her out evenings for joyous occasions together.

But Isabelle had passionate longings to which her husband seemed unresponsive. On their honeymoon, their first groping attempts to have sexual intercourse had been disappointing. They had not failed completely, but Isabelle felt let-down.

Her frustration grew deeper as the first two years of their married life passed. When they were in bed together she would often have ardent feelings that led her to snuggle close to her husband and to caress him. But almost always he failed to respond. Isabelle began to be afraid that her advances might build up resentment on his part. So she began to restrain herself. A chasm of coldness seemed to be deepening between them.

Her disappointment was not merely that their bodily partnership was not working out with the fervor and ecstasy of which she had dreamed. She longed deeply to have children. This had been her lifelong hope. Her husband seemed to hold aloof from any approach to this desire of hers.

The Joneses were members of a large church whose pastor was quite active in marriage counseling. One day Isabelle sought an appointment and poured out her difficulties. At first it was hard for him to tell what the real trouble was, but sympathetic and understanding questioning soon opened the floodgate of her disappointment and frustration.

At the pastor's suggestion, Isabelle asked her husband to make an appointment for a conference. When Edgar and the pastor were alone together in his study, the pastor asked him: "How much do you love your wife?"

"Oh, I love her very deeply!" Edgar replied. "We have a wonderful life together. She means everything to me."

But when the pastor, gently but persuasively, opened up the question of sex relations, Edgar flushed, stammered, and looked away. For a moment it seemed as though he would get up and leave. Friendly questioning finally opened up an episode that Edgar realized had played a major part in his own attitudes toward sex. As an adolescent he had had a puppy-love affair with a girl four years older than himself. This girl had been aggressive in a rather skillful way, and had led him on into an ardent attachment. One evening when he and she were alone in the parlor of his parents' home, she encouraged him to turn off the lights, and led him on into a quite passionate petting party. Just at the moment when he was engaging in the most intimate caresses he had ever experienced, his mother came into the room and turned up the lights.

Edgar had been emotionally deeply dependent on his mother. The shock of her stern disapproval and reproach came back over him with shame and self-condemnation whenever he thought about a woman's body. When he and Isabelle were in bed together he wanted to caress her. He sensed her longing to have him make love to her, but every time he felt a touch from her body he could see his mother standing beside the bed looking sternly at him, and his loving impulses were blocked and chilled.

The pastor listened understandingly to the story of this psychic wound that Edgar had suffered. He encouraged him to talk about it freely and fully. Then he asked a question:

"How much do you want to save your marriage from disaster?" he asked.

Edgar was startled. He had no idea that disaster threatened his marriage. Gently but unrelentingly the pastor helped him understand how vital it was to Isabelle that they should establish normal sex relations and should have children. Edgar objected: "You're right, undoubtedly. But this isn't something subject to my voluntary control. These attitudes of mine overwhelm me, out of this past experience with my mother. How can you reverse something that happened 12 years ago?"

"You can reverse it if you will learn to use deep prayer," the pastor told him.

Edgar said that he certainly wanted to, if only he could learn how. The pastor first taught Edgar how to relax physically and emotionally to a depth of serene detachment that he had never achieved before. Then he gave him these instructions:

> At the first opportunity, go off by yourself, in a comfortable place where you won't be interrupted, sit down in an easy chair and relax to this same deep serenity that you have now achieved. Then, in that state of profound relaxation, say to yourself: "Next

time my wife and I are together in bed I will hear
my mother say, 'Edgar, you love your wife. I want
you to make her happy. I want you to make love to
her. I want you to give yourself to her, heart and
soul and body. That is the right and only thing to do.
Make love to your wife with all your heart and all
your might.' "

Then you will stop thinking about your mother
and start thinking about how wonderful it is to express
physically your love for Isabelle.

Edgar carried out the pastor's instructions to the letter. Next
time Isabelle met the pastor she blushed clear up to the roots
of her hair and looked away. Then she looked at him gravely
and said: "Thank you, pastor!"

Within a year, the Joneses had a son. Within five years they
had three children. Their marriage had not only been saved; it
had been lifted to a new level of rapture and of creative partnership.

A pastor's family neared wreckage for lack of a budget

Not all ministers are experts on family matters, especially
when the problem concerns the minister's own family. A few
years ago, a marriage counselor in a Midwestern city had been
consulting with a recently-married young man about a problem
which, under her guidance, he had worked out with satisfying
success. Then he came back to the counselor with this question:

"Mrs. Brown, do you think you can help my father and
mother not to get a divorce?"

Under questioning, the young man told this story. His father
was a minister who was struggling along on a very moderate
salary. He had a wife, and a daughter who was attending high
school. The minister had old-fashioned ideas about family
finances. He had always taken it for granted that since the man
of the family was the one who earned the money, the man was
therefore the one who should maintain control over how the

money was spent. From his monthly salary he doled out funds to his wife, and occasionally to his daughter, but he kept telling them how limited their financial resources were, and he kept criticizing their expenditures even for necessary clothing and household equipment. As a result, some bitter quarrels had ensued and the question of divorce had been discussed.

The young man was concerned, first of all because he loved both his father and mother, and he felt that a divorce would be a disaster to them, to his sister, and to himself. Beyond that, he felt that a divorce would be a scandal in the church, and might quite possibly result in his father losing professional standing and make him unable to earn even the small amount of income he had been receiving.

Mrs. Brown asked whether the father and mother would come in to be interviewed, and they both appeared on the next day. First, Mrs. Brown interviewed the pastor. He took a rather stiff and self-righteous attitude, and attempted to justify the need for someone to keep a firm hand on family expenditures; he told of what he felt were the extravagances of his wife and daughter. Mrs. Brown asked him to wait outside and then interviewed the wife.

The wife broke down and wept during the interview. She told how her husband had invested money in books, for which he had no urgent need, at the very time when the family washing machine had become completely useless, and when he had just refused to help her finance a new one. She said that in most things they got along very well. They agreed in their religious ideals. They both were enthusiastic about their church work. They both loved their son and daughter deeply. The marriage was essentially sound, but the home was in imminent danger of being destroyed by the problems of family finances.

After consulting further with each of them, Mrs. Brown called the pastor and his wife in together. Under friendly discussion it developed that there were certain expenditures for which the pastor ought naturally to take responsibility—such as the monthly payments on his insurance, the bills for gasoline and car repairs, his own clothing, and some other items. On the other hand, they both agreed that she was the one who ought to take responsibility for buying the groceries, buying her own and the daughter's clothes and the household furnishings, paying the electric, gas and telephone bills, and some other items. It was agreed that the daughter's spending should be worked out in consultation between her and her mother.

After some discussion, both the pastor and his wife agreed on certain definite amounts to be set aside monthly for these expenditures, and they agreed that each should receive, on pay day, the total needed to cover his or her responsibilities. A moderate surplus was available beyond these budgeted needs. They both agreed that it would be fair to divide this surplus among the three of them—40 per cent to the father, 40 per cent to the mother, and 20 per cent to the daughter. And they both agreed that by following this plan it should be possible for the minister and his wife to establish a friendly partnership, even in financial matters. Then the counselor made a parting suggestion:

> As a minister, you are far more learned in these matters than I am, so that what I am about to say is offered to you quite diffidently. But I do feel that I ought to tell you a little about the experience of several of my clients who have discovered that the way out of family difficulties can quite often be found by means of what we call "the triangle of brotherly prayer."

Then she told the couple what she meant, and she explained also the techniques of listening prayer and deep prayer.

The pastor was silent for a minute. Then he said: "During all of my pastoral life I have been teaching to others that religion has the real answers to life's problems. I confess with some shame, and with real repentance, that I have failed to apply my own teachings. Thank you with all my heart for having shown me how religion can be put to work in changing our own family life from purgatory into something more really approaching heaven on earth."

HOW TO MOVE OUT OF PURGATORY
TOWARD PARADISE

After the honeymoon's romantic love has begun to fade into
the light of common day, and after the problems of sharing the
same bathroom, the same breakfast table, the same bed, and the
same bank account have begun to crowd in with little and large
frustrations and annoyances, many a marriage begins to develop feelings closely akin to purgatory. Where are the un-
marred raptures promised in the fairy-tale punch-line: ". . . and
then they lived happily ever afterwards"? This is the stage at
which many young married people begin to think of their
spouse as "that ball and chain."

Here is where our formula should come in, with its recon-
structive power. If a marriage has menacing developments, then
the creative response is to turn menace into promise by courage, to cooperate creatively, and to adventure spiritually. Let
us now get practical about it: Let us put down, one after another, the definite things that the husband and the wife each
need to do if they are seriously determined to carry out that
fundamental promise: "Come what may, I will seek thy joy!"

Remove needless irritants

Did you ever happen to run a small thorn or sliver into the
end of one of your fingers? Perhaps you didn't even notice when
it happened. But every time you touched something with that
finger there was a tiny stab of pain. It kept irritating. If you
neglected it, the spot began to be inflamed, and in a day or two
a little pus pocket formed around the thorn or the sliver. In
much the same way, small irritants in marriage relationships
may become like "a thorn in the flesh." The sensible thing to
do is to get rid of them, to eliminate needless irritants. These
irritants can develop on any one of the five basic levels of your
personality.

On the material level, financial arrangements can be irritating. That is what nearly wrecked the minister's marriage,

about which you were reading a few moments ago. Ask yourself: "What features about my own family finances are likely to cause needless irritation to my partner?" The wife may well ask herself whether she is extravagant or wasteful in her expenditures. Does she carelessly overdraw the bank account? Does she neglect to pay the bills even when there is money in the bank?

The husband may well ask whether he is domineering about family finances. Does he humiliate his wife needlessly by making her beg for money to run the household? Is he generous to himself about his own personal luxuries and then sharply critical about his wife's expenditures?

On the biological level, the husband may well ask himself whether he makes sexual demands on his wife in inconsiderate ways. Does he fail to use the gentle and loving courtship methods that are so much more satisfying than abrupt and self-centered demands?

Food also is biological. The wife may well ask herself whether she ever becomes negligent and thoughtless about serving the kinds of food her husband likes best, and serving it in ways that please him most. The husband may well ask himself whether he expresses warm appreciation often enough when his wife takes pains to cook his favorite dishes and to serve food just the way he likes it.

Needless psychological irritants are among the most abundant sources of marital unhappiness. Have you formed the habit of criticizing your marriage partner? Almost everyone feels hurt when people criticize in a harsh, unfriendly, persistent way. The nagging wife, the superciliously critical husband—such marriage partners can be truly maddening. Love your partner as is. Don't try to make him or her over.

Do you ever catch yourself criticizing your wife's (or your husband's) family? Do you ever needlessly criticize your partner's religion? Do you ever give your partner an excuse for feeling that you are domineering?

One word of warning is called for here. When any such list of needless irritants is read off, it is easy for the one who reads them to pounce upon the items in which the reader feels that his or her marriage partner is needlessly irritating. But no escape from purgatory is likely to be achieved merely by starting a new campaign to get your *partner* to be less irritating. The really hopeful and promising move is for you yourself to take a frank inventory of the ways in which *you* are irritating your partner needlessly. Then, without talking about it and without ostentation, start with vigor to eliminate the irritants for which you yourself are responsible.

Be appreciative

The familiar distinction between a pessimist and an optimist has important applications toward achieving marital happiness. The pessimist (you will remember) focuses all his attention on the *hole* in the doughnut, while the optimist sees and rejoices in the *doughnut*. Almost every wife and almost every husband has weaknesses, shortcomings, occasionally irritating habits. But almost every wife and husband has also a good many admirable, lovable, helpful, comforting qualities. The difference between a marriage that is headed for the rocks, and a marriage that is building solid joy and shared achievement, depends quite largely upon whether the two partners each focus their attention on the joy-producing qualities of their mate. "Accentuate the positive!" is the wise injunction of a song that won deserved popularity a few years ago.

Build friendliness systematically

When a good salesman approaches a prospective purchaser he always keeps in mind the importance of establishing friendly relations with the prospect. To ask him some friendly questions, to do him some little favor, to exchange a joke or two (or at any rate a friendly smile)—these are generally recognized as of major importance in establishing the cordial relationships on which business dealings are usually based. But if this systematic and thoughtful cultivation of friendliness is a good technique for salesmen, why not apply it to family relations?

How to double your marital happiness at small cost

Some years ago I was consulted by a wife who was facing a major crisis in her marriage because of needless and morbid feelings of guilt. She learned to triumph over this difficulty by means of deep prayer. A year later I had dinner at their home. When her husband was out of the room, I asked her whether her freedom from the guilt feelings had lasted. She said:

"Yes, it's all gone. That old disaster no longer threatens. Our marriage is on a much safer basis.

"But one thing troubles me," she blurted out. "My husband is gentle, and kind, and generous. But he's so awfully unexciting! Life gets so drab and ordinary sometimes."

Then she went on to list a series of complaints that she herself recognized were quite minor and subordinate.

When the husband came back into the room and the wife went into the kitchen to finish getting the dinner, I asked him a question: "How would you like to double your marital happiness at almost negligible cost?" The husband seemed startled, but he expressed interest in the idea. So I said to him:

Here are four rules. If you will follow these rules faithfully, I think I can practically guarantee that you will notice a major surge in the happiness of your married life:

1. At least once a week, buy your wife a small gift— a little bouquet of flowers, a box of candy, a copy of her favorite magazine, or perhaps a bit of costume jewelry.

2. Find fresh and heartwarming ways of telling your wife that you love her. Invent new kinds of caresses (being careful, of course, to choose ones that will thrill rather than annoy her).

3. Have a regular night each week when you take your wife out for two or three hours of happiness together—a movie, a dance, a little dinner, or whatever kind of treat you know will particularly appeal to her.

4. At least once a week—perhaps on Saturday after-

noon, or some other convenient time—say to your wife: "Darling, I have a couple of hours to spare. Isn't there something I can do for you around the house?"

Two weeks later I received a letter from this wife. She expressed a radiant surprise. Suddenly her marriage had been transformed!

Sometime later I was lecturing in another city to a woman's club. I told them about the four rules by which a husband could double his marital happiness. In the question period, one of the women asked: "What are the four rules by which a *wife* can double the happiness of *her* married life?" These are the four rules with which I answered her question:

1. Don't nag! Every woman carries around in her mouth a weapon with which she can wound and torture her husband—namely, her tongue. Stop using that weapon with the idea of reforming your husband.

2. Keep surprising him at mealtimes with the dishes which you know that he thinks are most delicious.

3. Respond to his sexual advances with understanding love and affection. If there are times when you have to deny his immediate wishes, make sure that you do it gently, and that you make him understand that it is a mere postponement of what will be welcomed and joyously shared as soon as conditions are more favorable.

4. Study the ways in which you can make it easier for your husband to succeed more fully on his job, in his business, or in his profession. Don't try to tell him how to do his work; just be his helpmate, his source of encouragement, inspiration, and (whenever possible) assistance.

Form family plans jointly

The marriage ceremony says that a husband and wife "become one flesh." That is vitally important. But it is also highly important that they learn to be of one mind. Differences of opinion are almost certain to emerge in marriage. When husbands and wives disagree about what they want to do or ought to do, this clash of ideas may breed resentment and suffering. But almost any difference of opinion can be transformed into an effective working agreement if the following rules are followed:

1. Be a good listener. In most family squabbles, the husband and the wife each loudly and aggressively seek to state his or her own point of view, paying very little understanding or attention to what the other person is saying. If you and your marriage partner get into controversies of that kind, use deep prayer to preset your own attitude, so that when differences of opinion arise, your basic reaction will be to try to understand your partner's point of view. Encourage your partner to talk. Ask sympathetic and understanding questions. Stop trying to convert your partner, and make sure that first of all you really put yourself in his or her place, and try to see things through his or her eyes.

2. Find areas of agreement. If you have listened understandingly, you will discover that you and your partner really share a great deal in what you want to accomplish, and even in your ideas about how those goals can be reached.

3. Surrender non-essentials. Suppose that you disagree with your partner about certain small points that seem important to him or her but that are not vital to you. Give in on those points. Do it generously and handsomely!

4. Agree to postpone controversial questions that do not need to be settled now. Theoretical questions about politics, or theology, or labor relations, or race relations (or what have you) can be debated almost endlessly, but do not have to be settled today or tomorrow. If you and your life partner have different opinions about such matters, just agree, in a friendly spirit, that you will disagree about those matters without trying to convert each other.

5. Find some creative program of action on which you and your partner can agree and can cooperate wholeheartedly. The plan does not have to be an *ultimate* solution of the problem. All that is needed is a practical cooperative working program

on which you can be friendly partners during the next week or two. Working together often brings hearts and minds together. If you can cooperate with mutual friendly helpfulness for a few weeks, or even a few days, you can then call another family council, talk things over once more, agree on another cooperative working program, and go forward for the next few weeks or days.

6. Use listening prayer and deep prayer to change your own attitudes when they need changing. If you find yourself feeling resentful, antagonistic, or destructively critical, or if you discover that your attitudes in any other way are interfering with creative partnership in your family, then take the very earliest opportunity to apply the spiritual skills that you have been developing in finding the path on which the Inner Light shines, and in gaining the divine courage and inspiration to follow that path.

WISE COUNSELING IS A VITAL PART OF CHRISTIAN MINISTRY

Almost everyone can gain new wisdom and new courage by talking out his or her problems with some wise and understanding counselor. During recent years, marriage counseling has become a widely recognized specialty. In most of our large cities professional marriage counselors are available, to be consulted on a self-respecting fee basis. Their wealth of past experience and of specialized professional training make them able to aid the formation of wise plans by those who consult them.

The social work counselor approaches marriage problems largely in the light of social science. He has been trained in psychology and sociology. Such counselors should be of major help in aiding any troubled person to grapple courageously and to cooperate creatively.

But above and beyond courage and cooperativeness lie the infinite resources of the spiritual adventure. Superhuman guidance and power are to be found with the aid of true religion. Here is the function of the minister, the rabbi, the priest. More and more, these spiritual advisors are being trained to bring the resources of religion to bear upon daily human life. If you are in need of spiritual counseling, explore the question of whether your pastor may be able to give you the kind of help you need. If you are a minister, it is well to ask yourself whether you are fulfilling adequately this counseling function of your ministry.

LOVE IN THE FAMILY LEADS US MORE FULLY INTO THE FAMILY OF GOD

When you and I were born to this earthly life, we were given a magnificent assignment. These physical bodies of ours are loaned to us as temporary habitations in order that we may gather a harvest of experience, and particularly in order that we may learn to live lovingly. To learn to share the lives of our fellow human beings, to learn to team up in the cooperative activities through which human life grows richer and richer— these are the basic tasks that are assigned us by virtue of the fact that here and now we are alive.

The nearest approach to ecstasy that most human beings achieve is the love that leads to marriage and parenthood. Here, in these most intimate relations between husband and wife and between parents and children, we have a God-given laboratory in which we may practice the basic skills for the gaining of which we have been sent upon this spiritual quest. Let us not miss this superb opportunity. Let us make use of all the resources that social science and spiritual wisdom can provide, in order that we may learn how to love each other truly, and how, out of that love, we may find fulfillment of life for each other and increasingly for the humanity of which we are a part.

SUMMING UP THE REMAKING OF MARRIAGE

Heaven begins at home. This chapter has given some working rules for transforming family life more and more into an effective unit of the Beloved Community.

"Come what may, I will seek thy joy!" is the real essence of the marriage vow. The following rules are practical aids toward putting that vow into full effect:

Remove needless irritants.
Build friendliness systematically.
Form family plans jointly. To do this effectively:
Be a good listener.
Find areas of agreement.
Surrender non-essentials.
Postpone theoretical controversies.
Team up on agreed working plans.
Use listening prayer and deep prayer to change your own attitudes when they need changing.

Wise counseling is a vital part of the Christian ministry.

Love in the family leads us more fully into the Family of God.

Chapter 13

How to Triumph

That fulfillment of life is the goal of religion, and that prayer can bring courage and joy have been keynotes of our shared thought in this book. But not all of life can be joyous. What can the spiritual venture do for you when really major menaces confront you?

Life calls for courage

All of us, at one time or another, have to face such menaces. Sooner or later, like almost everyone else, you must meet the day when someone close to your heart ceases forever to smile out from that earthly body which has been so dear to you. You may sometime have to live through days on which you realize that, though you have put forth what you believe to be your most strenuous and dedicated efforts, your achievements seem heartbreakingly less than you had hoped to attain. The day may come when someone whom you have trusted deeply, someone to whom you have given warm affection and devotion, turns out, in spite of everything, to seem to be unworthy. In matters of money, days may quite possibly come when your funds ebb so low that the golden dreams that you have dreamed are found to have been mirages. On such days, or on any other kind of

171

day when the reality that you must face turns out to be menacing, what can the spiritual adventure hold for you?

THE BACKGROUND OF THE ANSWER

Some of the vital principles by which life's tragedies, disappointments, and defeats can be met triumphantly have already
appeared in earlier pages of this book. Let us bring them to
mind once more, so that their power may be focused directly
on these sufferings of daily life that must be met and solved.

Fulfillment of life is the goal of religion

To adventure spiritually is not to surrender the richness of
life at its best, nor to sink back into grim pain and privation.
The Apostle Paul had endured his full share of suffering, perse-
cution, and hardship when he wrote to the Galatians:

> The harvest of the Spirit is love, joy, peace, good
> temper, kindliness, generosity, fidelity, gentleness, self-
> control.

Note that Paul bracketed together the harvest of joy and the
spiritual discipline through which that joy is achieved.

Good projects require hardships

Fulfillment of life, which is the goal of religion, is achieved
by losing yourself creatively in projects greater than yourself.
A good project not only stirs deeply the emotional energies,
and not only creates lasting values, but also involves hardships,
pain, suffering, danger—and even sometimes failure. The battle
is not worth winning unless it has to be *won*. Therefore, when
we encounter in our projects experiences that might bring
anguish, we can regain courage and press forward in creative
living by saying to ourselves: "Oh yes! Here are those difficulties that are so vital a part of every true project. By God's grace
and in His power we will turn the menace into promise, by the
courage and the creative love that are available through deep
prayer!"

GOD-GIVEN COURAGE TURNS LIABILITIES INTO ASSETS

Courage brings joy

One way to think of courage is to regard it as an indirect method of gaining joy in the long run. By meeting our problems courageously, we have far more chance of solving them, of getting rid of the menaces that have threatened us, and of the damages that may have been giving us pain and hardship.

But there is a much more direct and immediate way in which God-given courage means joy. Remember that courage, comradeship and creative faith are each of them ways of using our energies creatively instead of destructively. When the energy took the form of worry, fear, resentment, self-pity, anger, discouragement and despair, these destructive misdirections of our emotions were painful and even agonizing. But the moment that the energy is redirected into the creative and constructive channels that listening prayer and deep prayer open up, the dynamic flow begins to become inherently pleasant, happy, and joyous. We do not have to wait for a far-off reward, by and by. With God's help, the storm clouds begin to break up at once. His strength, His guidance, His courage, and His joy are ours *now*.

Gaining benefits from failure

The right use of deep prayer can cure you of being depressed. You need never again give way to discouragement, disheartenment, resentment, or self-contempt. But if you succeed in thus banishing emotional depression from your life, you need to develop a healthy substitute for the services that unawakened people obtain from the experience of getting depressed.

Of those who have not gained skill in deep prayer, the great majority swing up and down between enthusiastic self-confidence and more or less deep self-doubt. This fluctuation helps people to keep their balance. To have too long a run of luck is extremely likely to make the lucky person overconfident. This is likely to plunge the rashly confident person into disaster, and in the disaster-bath the egotistical over-confidence is purged away, so that the person can go back to work with a more even balance between confidence and caution. But if you have learned not to become depressed, then you, like the rest of us, are in urgent need of a good balance-wheel to keep down the rashness that otherwise might wreck our lives. This balance-wheel is provided by our confronting sanely our failures, misfortunes, and mistakes.

Let your failures teach you and prod you

The only people who never fail are the people who never dare. When you fail, say to yourself: "This seeming disaster can teach me much!" Take it deep into listening prayer. In your state of relaxation ask yourself:

"What was I really trying to achieve?"

"What can I learn from this failure?"

"What other ways are there by means of which I could achieve what I really wanted to achieve here?"

If you will listen attentively, and in deep relaxation, for answers to such questions as those, you are likely to find a flood of new insight coming to you, and that insight may be priceless. Then, if you still lack courage to make use of what you have learned, go into deep prayer and get God's help to try again more wisely and with better understanding.

Bereavement can be triumphed over by deathless life and love

Death can have no victory over those who are fully awakened to the spiritual life. Our loved ones who go on before us into the wider world are still our spiritual companions. And we ourselves can live on into the years with serene courage, knowing that when Death comes he will prove to be a great friend, opener of the gateway into life more magnificent.

Brotherhood can take the sting out of misfortune

Suffering that is shared often finds an antidote in the very process of sharing. One of the most pervasive keynotes of the New Testament is brotherly love. Of the writers in the New Testament, one of those who laid the greatest stress on brotherhood was the Apostle John. In his First Epistle he wrote these great words:

> We know that we have passed out of death into life because we love the brethren.

Many of life's seeming menaces can be turned into blessings by following these rules:

1. Use deep prayer, giving full attention to the step of reconciliation.

2. Look around you for others who are facing problems similar to your own. Follow the Apostle Paul's advice: "Rejoice with those who rejoice, and weep with those who weep."

3. Team up with others to solve shared problems. Use creative discussion and use the triangle of brotherly prayer.

The Power above all human power can help you meet your problem

If alcoholics who have literally drunk themselves into the gutter, or into the delirium-tremens ward, can rise up with triumphant strength by throwing themselves upon the power of God, then surely this same divine resource is available to all of us if we will seek it in our times of need. Never submit to any ultimate defeat. If you use listening prayer and deep prayer truly and fully, then a pathway to courage, to service, and to triumphant living is always to be found.

HE HAD NEEDED MONEY

Edgar Cunningham came into my office one spring day. He said that he was on a spiritual quest and wanted to talk it over. He was following an inner light, seeking further guidance.

This had been his experience. He had worked his way up to an executive position in an industrial plant. As a result of his mother's teaching during his boyhood, and as the outgrowth of a series of experiences that had come to him in the church in which he was active, he had made some practical discoveries about the power of prayer.

He learned to win comrades and partners

For example, before he went into a conference about a difficulty in the labor relations of the plant, he would first put a "Do Not Disturb" sign on his office door, tell the switchboard not to send in any phone calls, and then he would sit down in an especially comfortable chair that he kept for the purpose. He would open his heart to God, laying before Him the problem with which he was about to come to grips. He would see how he could put himself in the place of each of the other men who were to take part in the conference. He would pray only to be guided in the pathway of understanding and of creative teamwork.

Then he would go into the conference, and he would make it his business to be a good listener. He would draw out the views, the needs, and the ideas of his associates. He would keep asking friendly and understanding questions until the real problem began to come fully into view. He would wait with open mind and open heart until a lead toward a creative solution would come into his mind. Then he would seek to develop that solution with the fullest attainable cooperation of all concerned.

This method had proved amazingly successful. Problems that at first seemed insoluble gave way, and turned into forward surges of success for the firm. Cunningham became convinced that he was in contact with a real Power, a source of wisdom higher than any human wisdom. He felt a deep eagerness to spend the rest of his life learning more about that Power.

But his financial problems demanded a spiritual solution

He had a wife and four children to support. He loved them deeply, and wanted to make it possible for his wife to live the sort of life to which she aspired, and to provide for his children every opportunity to grow into the finest men and women they were capable of becoming. He faced the problem of how to find a legitimate source of income that would provide for his family and that would thus set him free for his spiritual quest.

Then he realized that this problem could be solved by the same essential method that he had been using in his factory conferences. He went to his office one morning very early, long before breakfast. He sat down in his comfortable chair, relaxed deeply, and laid his problem before the Higher Wisdom. Then an idea came to him, an idea that took possession of him and kept growing. He would seek out some "sick" industrial company, a company that was engaged in manufacturing some needed and worthwhile product but that was being mismanaged, and that had dropped in its market value to a point far below its real potential worth. Then (with the aid of financial partners), he would purchase control of that establishment and would build it up by means of his method of spiritual guidance and friendly partnership. After the business had been restored to health, he would sell out his interest at its real value.

Spiritual aspirations found financial backers

He took this plan to some wealthy friends of his. One of them has an office in Radio City; another is associated with a famous Wall Street firm. Following his Inner Light, he laid his project before these men of wealth. Each of them agreed to make large resources available.

Cunningham then made a search for his "sick" industrial

establishment. He found it, and having consulted with his backers, they jointly purchased control. He then resigned from his old position and took over the management of the newly purchased company. Applying the methods of spiritual understanding and of creative good will that he had used in his previous position, he was able to work out cooperative solutions of the problems that had brought the company to the verge of bankruptcy. Production increased. Costs went down. The value of the stock moved upward.

The achievement exceeded his hopes

Cunningham had estimated that it would take five years for him to accumulate the resources needed to set him free from business cares, so that he might pursue his spiritual objective with all his heart, mind, soul, and strength. Actually, he achieved his financial goal in four years instead of five. He and his business partners sold their interest in the revived company. Everyone had gained; no one had lost. His partners said to him: "Now, of course, you'll go out and look for another sick establishment!" "Oh, no," he replied, "I have achieved my objective." And he walked out with a friendly smile, turning his back on their astonished faces.

When he came to my office, he was on his way back from Florida, where he had taken his family for a vacation. He had no financial worries. He came to me as one of several people from whom he sought suggestions as to the best way to invest the leisure that he had won, and thus to go forward in further spiritual exploration.

HOW TO BE HAPPY THOUGH POOR

That the right use of deep prayer and listening prayer can often result in major increases in the income of a truly religious person has just been pointed out in the case of Edgar Cunningham. But perhaps, when you take earnestly and wholeheartedly the steps of listening prayer, and when you thus seek an answer to your own financial or economic problems, there may come to you the clear realization that what you need to do is to stop worrying about getting more money, and to learn to make the best and fullest spiritual use of the income that is already being provided.

The matter can be stated in another way: As related to problems of poverty and wealth, your fulfillment of life will depend on two factors. The first factor consists in the income that you receive. This factor may be crucial. It is true that extreme poverty and privation may in themselves be damaging to life fulfillment. But the second—and by far the more important—factor consists in your attitude toward your income and your possessions, the use that you make of your resources, and even more significantly, your capacity to achieve joy and creative service through channels that do not depend upon wealth or income. It is to this second group of factors that we must turn our thoughts.

Devote yourself to the values that grow by being shared

Some of the things that many men and women value most highly in our civilization are those that grow less by being shared. Take, for example, an estate of $10,000 that is to be divided among a number of heirs. The more this money is shared, the less remains to the individual heir. Or, consider the supply of food and of drinking water in a lifeboat that is adrift after the sinking of a ship. The more these vital necessities are shared, the less food and water remain for the individual who does the sharing.

In general, material goods grow less by being shared. Where the material goods are limited and scarce, the more money, or land, or property, or jewels, or other material goods one gives away, the less one has left.

But consider some of the things that grow greater by being shared. Take, for example, knowledge. Anyone who is a teacher, and who puts his heart into his work, comes to realize that in the process of teaching he learns in a way that he never could have achieved without having shared his knowledge. The more truth you give away, the more you have left. The more insight, knowledge, wisdom, and intellectual inspiration you share, the more remains in your own mind and life. Truth grows by being shared.

Beautiful experiences can grow by being shared. If you call the attention of someone else to a wonderful sunset, you yourself are likely to enjoy the sunset more. If you help someone else to discover the beauties of spring flowers, or of children's faces, or of great music, your own appreciation of beauty is enhanced in these acts of sharing. The more you share the awareness of beauty, the more awareness you have left.

Or take comradeship. Here is something that you cannot achieve without sharing. To be sure, it is not always the largest group that achieves the greatest comradeship. But the degree to which you share life with companions, associates, and friends determines in large measure how much you receive. The greater the sharing, the greater the return. This is the secret of the Great Teacher: "Give, and you will have ample measure given you."

Love itself grows by being shared. True, it is possible to love silently and secretly. But when love is communicated, when it is given with all your heart, then it comes to fuller flower. It is the sharing of love with the beloved that best increases love.

Above all, spiritual insight grows greater by being shared. Try this experiment: In your next morning meditation, when you are deeply relaxed and dedicated, say to yourself:

> Today, you are to be watching alertly for any new spiritual insight that may come to you. And you are to be watching receptively for any outreaching by any person whom you may meet, who shows a hunger for such spiritual insight. Whenever the insight comes, you will welcome it and receive it to the full. And when any seeker reaches out toward you, you will respond openheartedly and with outgoing understanding.

Repeat that experiment on several different days. Make a note of what comes to you as a result of such meditation. You will find that when you seek to transmit your spiritual insights, they grow in vividness, depth, and splendor.

Find the costless ways to live life joyously

Building on the fundamental fact that the primary values of your life are to be those that grow by being shared, consider for a few moments the ways in which the stage can best be set for such shared experiences. Of course, there does have to be a stage. We live in physical bodies that move about in a physical world. And many of the physical facilities and resources that are used even in shared experiences carry a price tag. If our incomes are small and our material needs are great, how can we obtain the bare minimum material essentials for life fulfillment?

If you have never done this, try a brief experiment: Sit down and make as full a list as you can of the opportunities for shared experience that are available in your community without financial cost, or at very nominal expense. You might use the following checklist as a starter, writing down on a sheet of paper or in a notebook the specific details about opportunities of these sorts that are within range of your daily or weekly living:

What public library facilities are accessible to you? How long is it since you have visited your nearest public library? Have you obtained a card by means of which you can borrow books from that library?

Do the public schools offer evening classes in which you might be interested? How about classes at the YMCA or the YWCA? Are there colleges or universities in your city that offer courses at nominal or moderate charges? Or, if your intellectual ambitions are less strenuous, how about clubs in which current books are reviewed and discussed?

What record libraries or loan collections are there, and what facilities for playing such records are easily available to you?

What social centers are available where you might join one or more groups active along lines which appeal to you? What arts and crafts activities can you locate that would give outlets to your creative capacities? How about weaving, pottery, painting, clay modeling, needlework?

What singing society, choir, or musical club would be open to your membership if you sought the opportunity?

What groups interested in outdoor activities are open to your participation? Is there a hiker's club in your vicinity? Are there nature-study groups that you might enjoy? How about bird-watching? How about groups interested in collecting various kinds of minerals, or wild flowers? Is there a gardeners' club which you might join—if gardening interests you?

What civic groups are active in your community? Make a list of such groups, setting down the requirements for membership and the activities engaged in, and ask yourself which would be the one coming closest to providing you with an outlet for creative activity.

Are you a church member? If not, do you have a church home where you attend regularly? If you are not so attached, what churches are there within your easy access that specialize in activities that might express your own creative aspirations and your own spiritual outreachings?

What individuals in need of personal friendliness are within your reach? Are there blind people who need to have someone read to them? Are there boys or girls who need to be given opportunities to join with scout groups? Are there youngsters in danger of becoming delinquents or criminals who are in need of big-brother or big-sister leadership?

Make a list of agencies that need volunteer helpers. For example, veteran's hospitals have varied jobs for volunteer workers, and pediatrics wards have great need of women to amuse and feed small children. The Red Cross needs volunteers.

What are your own political affiliations? Have you made contact with the ward or precinct organizations of your party? If you are politically independent, what groups within your reach are interested in promoting the election of honest and efficient public servants, and in advocating such legislation as will best promote the public welfare?

ADVENTURE SPIRITUALLY IN A CHALLENGING WORLD

Our spiritual adventure is no mere fair-weather project. The real test, as to whether our spiritual vision and life are valid, comes when adversity stares us in the face. At moments that without a living and creative faith would be dark and anguished, we are challenged to test the reality and creative power of the superhuman resources that we have begun to use in our spiritual adventure. Ancient wisdom has said: "Man's extremity is God's opportunity." When defeat seems to press in upon you, when (if ever) you are tempted to think of yourself as contemptible, when physical, mental, and spiritual anguish seem to be too much to bear, then say to yourself: "Here is a chance to test out how real are the spiritual resources in which I have put my faith. Now, O Father, is my time of dire need. O God, help me!"

TRIUMPH CAN BE WON OVER PAIN, POVERTY, SUFFERING, AND EVIL

Here is the essence of this chapter:

Fulfillment of life is found through projects, but projects require hardships. Benefits can be gained from failure. Brotherhood can take the sting out of misfortune. Bereavement can be triumphed over by deathless life and love. And the Power above all human power can help you meet your problem.

Sometimes, as in the case of Edgar Cunningham, spiritual guidance can lead to major increases in income. Sometimes the spiritual gift is learning how to be happy on a very moderate income. This can be promoted by devoting yourself to the values that grow by being shared. Make an inventory of the costless ways to live life joyously. Adventure spiritually in a challenging world!

Chapter 14

How to Win the Truest Success

You want to succeed. Of course you do—every purposeful person goes through life building up in his mind pictures of what he wants to be and to do. Your daily struggle is to make these pictures come true. That is the daily struggle of every purposeful person. But—

WHAT DO YOU MEAN BY SUCCESS?

In seeking to bring these inner dreams and visions to realization, the character of your success depends upon two things: First, what kinds of dreams do you aspire to fulfill? Second, to what degree do you actually achieve fulfillment of those dreams? If you can solve those two questions, you can succeed truly.

Is money your measure of success?

In our Western world, success has come to be measured quite largely in terms of wealth and income. To many people, every rich man or woman is regarded as being successful, while everyone who fails to win financial ease is thought thereby really to have failed. If you measure success in terms of progressing from poverty toward material abundance, have you tested out the suggestions on that subject given in Chapter 13?

Do you measure success in terms of power?

Many people measure attainment in terms of climbing the ladder of promotion, of being able to give orders to more and more people, and to take orders from fewer and fewer superiors. Many a girl who looks forward to marriage measures her success in terms of the power that she can gain over men, the power to make them pay attention to her, the power to make them spend money in giving her good times, the power to make them fall in love with her and beg her to accept their love and their earthly goods.

Measuring success by fulfillment of life

That the goal of true religion is fulfillment of life has been indicated in Chapter 2. To live life deeply, fully, vividly, and richly is the truest success. It is possible to be extremely wealthy and still to find life empty, disappointing, painful, and miserable. It is possible to hold great power and still to live in fear, loneliness, and frustration. Gangsters and dictators gain great power, but generally fail to achieve fulfillment of life. Many a flirt has shown her power by breaking one heart after another, only to find at the end that her own heart is broken and her life shattered.

Success and your real ideals

In the final reckoning, no one but yourself can decide what are to be your ideals and aspirations. You, and only you, can do that.

Merchants sometimes make use of the slogan: "You, above all, must be satisfied." If that is true (in any degree) of merchandising, it is extremely true in relation to success. True success is not achieved until you, with all your heart, and with single-minded satisfaction, feel that you have achieved what you yourself, at your moments of clearest and highest vision, have aspired to achieve.

Use meditation to clarify your purposes

For this, you will do well to use simple intuition. Go apart into the quiet, comfortable, undisturbed place in which you are accustomed to pray. There, go through the process of deep and profound relaxation. But before you pray, come face to face with yourself. In the deep serenity of profound relaxation and single-minded concentration, ask yourself this question: "What do I really want out of life? Ten years from now—or in twenty or thirty years—what are the things that I shall have achieved and will have become that will cause me joy and satisfaction." When the answer to these questions begins to take shape in your mind, put these long-run purposes of yours into silent words. Say to yourself inwardly: "These are my goals in life; this is what I *really* want to attain. . . ." Then, after you have put these long-run purposes into silent words, open your eyes, take pen and paper, and write those same words down, clearly and simply, as a record to be kept.

WHAT ARE THE STEPS IN MAKING YOUR DREAMS COME TRUE?

Your first main step toward true success has been taken if you have clarified your own vision as to what you want to achieve. Once you know clearly, and with deep certainty, what your real goals are, the problem of success reduces to a question as to the means by which those ends can be achieved. Here are seven rules that you may find worth trying in this struggle to fulfill your dreams.

1. Fit your 5 per cent into the 95 per cent that needs you

One frequent source of failure is that the ambitious person quite often tries to impose his 95 per cent upon a reluctant world, being ready to concede only a 5 per cent adjustment on his part to the plans and purposes of other people. To illustrate this source of failure, let me cite an extreme case:

A man whom I will call Jocko Orlando became convinced that he had found the secret of how to save the world. His secret actually consisted in his discovery that he could get flashes of intuition by relaxing profoundly, by asking questions of his own unconscious mind, and by then listening attentively for the answers. Some of the flashes that he had gotten in this way were actually quite remarkable. But he had not learned how to check and correct his intuitive insights by means of common sense, science, and creative discussion. Instead, he was aggressively urging the rest of the world to accept him as leader.

He had been employed by an interstate trucking enterprise. He had worked there only a few months, but he went to an official of the company and offered to double the company's profits by making his intuitive powers available. When this offer was refused, he promptly resigned. He went to an aged uncle, and persuaded him to lend $10,000 out of his life's savings, persuading the uncle that Jocko's flashes of intuition would make it easy for him to win several million dollars in the stock market in a few weeks. He called in five of his personal friends, and offered to double their salaries if they would resign from their present positions, and become his assistants, with the proviso that they were to obey him instantly and unquestioningly, trusting to his intuition to bring success to all of them.

Such a case represents a pathological overdevelopment of self-confidence. But if you will make a quiet study of aggressive people whom you know, and who are failing, you will probably find that a good many of them are seeking to impose their ideas and their plans in wholesale ways on other people.

In contrast with the domineering aggressiveness of the egomaniac, you are likely to find the following to be a promising road toward success:

Take a modest but searching inventory of your own strengths, capacities, and resources. What do you have to offer that other people might find useful?

After you have an answer to that question, make a careful survey to discover who the people are who might find it useful and profitable to employ these resources of yours. After you have located some possible prospects, make a careful study of how you might most effectively make them aware of ways in which you could be useful to them. Next, take every reasonably sound and hopeful opportunity to be of service. Use your capacities in helping other people to carry out *their* plans. Fit yourself thoughtfully and considerately into their needs and purposes. Regard these activities as trial runs, in which you are gaining skill and experience by doing your very best to be of service to others.

If this general kind of program is carried forward, the chances are excellent that (probably quite unexpectedly, and from some source that you have not directly sought out) an opening for larger usefulness will be offered to you. When others seek your services and ask your help you are on a highly promising path toward success. But the degree of your success will be determined to a very great extent by your ability to fit your capacities, your skills, your experience, and your energy into the pattern of the plans and purposes of your employer, and of your associates.

This same general rule applies with equal effect if you are trying to succeed in making friends. Many people fail in their search for friendship because the seeker wants the other people to fit into his interests, to do what he wants them to do, to talk about the things which absorb his interests, and the other people seem not to care to be enlisted as means to his ends. If you want friends, become an expert at understanding other people's interests and needs. Keep leading into the other person's long suit. Join in the activities about which he is enthusiastic. Encourage him to talk about the things that are rousing his interest.

If and when other people seek to exploit you ruthlessly, this pattern of success does not call for acquiescing ignobly. Jesus himself said to his disciples:

"I am sending you out like sheep among wolves; so be wise like serpents and guileless like doves."

Your success will not be founded upon your becoming other people's slaves or doormats. But neither will true success come from egotistical domineering. What you need to achieve is creative partnership, fitting yourself into the patterns of reality, including the *mutually advantageous* patterns of other people's purposes. Cooperating creatively is the key to the highest achievement.

2. Be a promise, not a menace

The energies of our personalities are aroused by stimulus situations in which we find ourselves. These stimulus situations are mostly of two kinds—menacing and promising. If someone tries to domineer you, or criticizes you harshly, or is reckless with your property, or breaks his promises to you, you are likely to regard that person as a menace. If someone is friendly, understanding, admiring, cooperative, and helpful, you are likely to regard that person as a promising stimulus.

Now most people have fairly standardized ways of responding to these two kinds of situations. Most of us, when we meet the menacing stimulus, do one of two things—we try to escape from it and in future to avoid it, or we attack it and try to destroy its menacing possibilities. In other words, toward menacing stimulus situations, we are likely to react with such emotions as fear, aversion, anger, resentment, and antagonism. But when we meet a promising stimulus our reactions are likely to be enthusiasm, admiration, affection, and cooperativeness. If you encounter a promising stimulus you want to stay with it—or with him.

Now, to other people, *you* are a stimulus. In order to increase your chances of success, what sort of reactions do you want other people to give to your stimulating activities? The answer is fairly obvious. You want other people to like you, admire you, be enthusiastic about you, and cooperate with you. To get these reactions from other people, the formula is quite simple: be a promising not a menacing stimulus! If you find that people are reacting toward you as though you were a menace, the obvious and sensible thing to do is make a study of your own behavior and find out what sorts of attitudes and actions on your part are making them regard you thus. Change those behavior patterns so that you will be promising rather than menacing, and you will begin to get the kinds of reactions that you need and desire in order to achieve true success.

Of course, we have to live up to our promises if we want to go on being regarded as promising stimuli. Dependability, reliability, trustworthiness—these are not mere moral rules set up by some sour-faced policeman. These characteristics are essential elements in the social psychology of success.

3. Use deep prayer to change your own attitudes

Rule 2, about being a promise instead of a menace to your associates, sounds good until you actually try to put it into effect. Then you are likely to discover how hard it is to alter your own habitual patterns of behavior, even when you most earnestly desire to make them over.

The answer to this difficulty is to be found in deep prayer. Go back to Chapter 8, and to the other chapters that give instructions about this method of gaining superhuman help in living up to your own best ideals. The needed spiritual aid is awaiting your search.

4. Learn from your failures

Failure can be a precious thing. Yes, you read that correctly: a failure can be a precious thing. Roughly speaking, there are 99 wrong ways of doing anything for every one right way of doing it. When you are striving for success in some new undertaking, the chances of attaining that one right way on the first trial are relatively small. Even the wisest people often have to fail several times before they reach true success. Regard each unsuccessful attempt as one of the necessary steps on the road. Say to yourself: "Ah! There is one of the failures that I had to get through before I could truly succeed!"

A second way in which a failure can be truly precious is that it can rouse emotional energy which, if rightly directed, can be a main drive toward future success. Failures can be poisonous if they make you stop trying. But failures can give the challenging impact that drives you to making a better try next time.

A third way in which a failure may be a precious thing is that it can give you wisdom that cannot otherwise be gained. To succeed, you have to become familiar with your problem. You have to get the feel of your problem. You have to get to know what will happen if you do certain things. You have to learn what are the wrong things to do as well as what are the right things. You may be sadder for a few brief moments when you come out from failure, but you should certainly be wiser.

"But," you quite likely may object, "it's very hard to take failures that way. It is really extremely difficult to recognize the three ways in which a failure is precious."

True enough! And for that reason it is vitally important that you learn to take your failures to the Almighty in deep prayer. Carry through all the steps, up to the point where you, in deep relaxation, have invoked the divine presence. Then, out of the deep peace and reassurance of that holy place, make this prayer:

> **Father, teach me to make this failure precious in Thy service. All of the pain which it has brought is dedicated now to Thee. Stir me and prod me with this failure, O God, that I may move forward toward true success under Thy guidance.**

5. Release your fullest energies

To succeed fully, to the limit of your best possibilities, you need to be filled with inner power. You need to have energy flowing through your body, your heart, and your mind, energy that can be transmitted into enthusiasm, courage, and tenacious perseverance. You are not likely to succeed if you feel listless, bored, half-hearted, and discouraged.

To achieve this full and abundant flow of energy you need of course to follow a wise diet and to be in good health. You need also to be able to sleep soundly when the time has come for sleeping, and to be able to be wide-awake, alert, and energetic when the time has come to put forth your energies into efforts toward success. Healthy living, and full command of your own energy resources, are vitally important in order that you may truly succeed.

6. Let your vision of success keep growing

No explorer ever appreciates the full possibilities of a new territory when he first enters it. To explore is to find out, to discover, to open up what was previously unknown. You are exploring possibilities of true success. Your first venture should give you wider vision. The vision that you are trying to achieve can be enriched as soon as you have taken the first few steps toward realizing it.

This is true also of every worthwhile friendship. It is true certainly of every wise marriage. And it is abundantly true in any well-chosen employment to which you have set yourself. As the Bible puts it:

> They go from strength to strength. . . . The path of the righteous is like a dawning light that shines more and more. . . .

7. Succeed with God

Go back and read those three words again: "Succeed with God!" What does it mean? It might mean three different things. Indeed, it means all of these three combined together into a rich fulfillment:

First, "Succeed with God" means "Fulfill the steps that are necessary in order to achieve listening prayer and deep prayer to its fullest potential."

The second meaning of those three words is: "Bring your purposes into harmony with the will of God." The Almighty always succeeds. To be fully in harmony with Him becomes synonymous with success.

Third, Team up with God. Your humble purposes and my humble purposes, tiny as they may seem in cosmic perspective, are part of God's will, part of His design if we have brought our lives into alignment with His will. Thus, through deep prayer, we may become true partners with the Divine. His creative energy, flowing through us and through others, can bring to fulfillment events and achievements that would not have come to pass if you and I had not been actively seeking to live our lives as part of His life. The Creator makes use of us in the fulfillment of His own design. We find fulfillment by losing ourselves in His creativity.

SUMMING UP SUCCESS IN THE LIGHT OF THE SPIRITUAL ADVENTURE

The first step is to decide what you mean by success.

Is money your measure? Is it power? Or is it fulfillment of life? True success can be had only in terms of what are really your own ideals. Use meditation to clarify your purposes.

Seven rules are worth trying in your struggle to fulfill your purposes

1. Fit your 5 per cent into the 95 per cent that needs you.
2. Be a promise, not a menace.
3. Use deep prayer to change your own attitudes.
4. Learn from your failures.
5. Release your fullest energies.
6. Let your vision of success keep growing.
7. Succeed with God.

<hr/>

Chapter 15

Old Age, Faith, and Courage

Does this concern you?

This chapter is written for three special groups of people.

First it is for those who have already passed the age of 65 years, or who have retired from their chief past occupation, or have found that the major project of rearing children has either come to a close or has reached a major turning point because the children have left home.

A second group of people for whom this chapter is written is made up of those who have not yet reached the retirement age, but who begin to realize that middle life is slipping away, and that fairly soon the problems of the later decades must be faced.

The third group who may find needed help in this chapter are those who are still young, but whose parents or other loved ones are encountering the problems of the riper years, and might gain from guidance as to how to harvest the full richness of that potentially golden age.

PROJECTS CAN BRING FULFILLMENT
IN THE LATER YEARS

Life can be rich. It can have high and deep joy, and it can be satisfying, even at times when energy ebbs and the excitements

194

of youth seem far away. In a very special sense, the later decades should be a time of life fulfillment, a time when past struggles and striving bring their fruition and their reward. But empty lives are obviously not finding fulfillment. No healthy-minded person who has reached these years of high maturity with a normally healthy body wants to be settled permanently into a rocking chair, and be told to fold his hands and be quiet. Like the earlier decades of life, these senior years must have their projects, their activities that rouse keen interest and enthusiasm, that have difficulties to be surmounted, and that produce creative results. No impassable barrier to creative adventure need be set up at the age of 65, nor at any other terminus of the middle years. Life brings its growing harvest of experience and wisdom. It can bring a richer and richer harvest of satisfaction, of joy, and of productivity.

Hardships may have to be met

Every good project has hardships that must be overcome. We have seen in earlier chapters that that is an essential feature for life-fulfillment. In our riper years there is assigned to us the project of growing old—not only gracefully and gently, but triumphantly, mounting new heights of experience and perhaps even new peaks of achievement. What, then, are the special difficulties that are presented to us in this task of making the riper years the richest?

Financial difficulties stand out

To retire from the occupation in which you have earned your living means, naturally, that the earnings cease. Even when retirement allowances become available, they rarely form more than a minor fraction of what the full earnings used to be. Moreover, children who have been living at home and contributing to the family income, quite often get married and have their own families and households to support. How can these financial stresses be resolved? Let us consider some practical suggestions:

If you are still in the stages of looking forward to old age, one of the wise and prudent things to do is to work out, at the earliest practicable age, a sensible program for taking care of the financial needs of the later years. Several rules apply here. First, save wisely. Life insurance, bonds, savings accounts, and other investments that produce fixed incomes are subject to being shrunken painfully and even disastrously by the rising cost of living. Investments in wisely selected stocks and real estate produce incomes that tend to increase if, as, and when the cost of living increases. But everyone has his own special problems in this field of saving and investment. The crucial need is to plan with the aid of the wisest and most trustworthy advice that you can get.

Early in life it is a great idea to make sure that your earning power will continue after you reach the age of 65. Perhaps you can select an occupation where no old-age deadline cuts off your employment. Or perhaps you can build up one or more profitable sidelines of activity, by means of which you can earn money even after you are retired from what has been your main occupation. Various kinds of insurance schemes are developing, by means of which a home and adequate care can be provided during declining years. Such plans need (of course) to be studied thoroughly before you invest in them.

But let us suppose that you are already in the later decades, and that you have been unable to lay aside financial resources adequate to give you comfort after your main income stops. In that case, life has assigned you this project:

Achieve the joy that defies financial limitations!

Find out how to be happy though poor. One of the first things to do in working on that project is to apply listening prayer. You will need to do that repeatedly. Then, by means of listening prayer and also by means of consultation and experimentation, find out whether there are ways in which you can earn outside income to help relieve the worst shortages. Next, if you find it necessary to live with your married children or with other people, use listening prayer and deep prayer as aids in achieving friendly cooperation and mutual helpfulness in the task of joyous living. Chapter 13 on "How to Triumph [over Pain, Poverty, Suffering, and Evil]" has suggestions that will be appropriately helpful.

Finding the channels for creative activity

Other things besides loss of financial income may bring hardship in the later years. There is the problem of possible loss of challenging activities, and of life-enriching contacts with fellow workers. Many a retired person feels a painful decline of prestige and importance.

To find activities that make life worth living, and to build up friendly contacts with other people—these are exactly the kind of things where listening prayer and deep prayer are powerful aids. The next two sections outline some kinds of projects which, if explored to the full, may provide the means to change the later decades of your life from drab, dreary, disappointed loneliness to a fine flowering of creative activity.

Remember that old age has certain major assets that are denied to other periods of life. Persons in these golden decades have usually been relieved of the responsibilities of rearing small children. They are no longer tied down to a time-clock, nor to the responsibility of getting children off to school and the husband off to work. Now is the time to do the things you always wanted to do but for which you lacked the opportunity. Make it your basic project in these liberated years to meet the problems of later life with full employment of the Three Do's. *Do* grapple courageously with old-age problems; *do* cooperate in fellowship with others who face similar problems; and *do* adventure spiritually in the process.

Popular magazines have been featuring some of the projects in which older people, through courage, have been turning

the menace of old age to promise, who find in their comrades
and partners a stimulus to creativeness. Some of the trailer
camps in the South, particularly in Florida and in California,
have developed community life in which people who have
reached full maturity live with joyous fellowship and with rich
creative leisure. In many Northern cities, Golden Age clubs
have been organized in which people in these later decades
get together for recreation, for fellowship, and for shared activities to enrich each other's lives.

Not long ago *Look* magazine applauded *Senior Achievement,
Inc. Look,* in its issue of April 17, 1956, described the project
thus:

> It is providing job opportunities for retired men
> and women over 65 years of age. A Chicago organiza-
> tion, *Senior Achievement* is financed by industry and
> foundation grants. It helps give older people employ-
> ment service. In one of the workshops, they do wood,
> textile and metal work; in the other, they package fine
> foods and candies, and do drafting work for Chi-
> cago firms. Through its employment service, *Senior
> Achievement* provides executive, engineering, clerical
> and custodial help for offices on a contract basis. The
> workers put in four to five hours a day, earn no more
> than the $1,200-a-year maximum income permitted
> [up to 72] without impairing their Social Security
> benefits. One 77-year-old lady reflects the busy group's
> spirit this way: "Sitting home in a rocking chair—
> that's for vegetables, not for people."

Another possibility is this:

Seniors can create their own friendly community

Let them develop a project in which persons who have retired from the toilful obligations of middle life undertake, first,
a survey of the population over 60 years of age; second, the
organization of committees of older people for the purpose of
setting up a community program for the riper years, and, third,
the publication of a mimeographed sheet by means of which

people in these age groups can share the news about one another and can get together for mutually helpful activities. Through these channels, a program of mutual visitation may be developed, so that persons who are bedridden or housebound can enjoy fellowship, and can share in the common stream of the rich experience of their fully mature fellows.

Having a healthy old age

To stay fully healthy in the later years is an important part of this project. Some of the physical ills which are likely to develop in the later years can be cured or alleviated by the medical wisdom that geriatric specialists are beginning to develop and apply. Even more important is the cultivation of healthy attitudes of mind and spirit. Deep prayer can be a powerful help toward achieving the ideal of a healthy mind in a healthy body.

SHE THOUGHT SHE HAD CANCER, BUT SHE NEEDED A PROJECT

A woman had very successfully raised to manhood and womanhood a son and a daughter. While her children were in the later stages of growing up, she had combined wifehood, motherhood, and a career: she had served as full-time secretary with an executive officer of a large advertising firm in New York City. Her son was in law school in another city and her daughter, in still another city, was studying to be a librarian. This left her more time to devote to her professional activities, and to a number of civic responsibilities that she had undertaken in church organizations and in the League of Women Voters.

At this juncture, her husband received an attractive offer to become district manager in a distant city. Since this seemed to be of vital importance to him, the wife moved with him to the new location, not only cheerfully but joyfully. She quite happily decided to retire from the professional work that had occupied her outside her home.

For six months she sat around in her new residence, watching television soap operas, reading murder mysteries, and thinking about her friends and previous activities back in New York City. As yet she had made only a few friends, and these on a relatively superficial basis. She was not the kind of person who could be happy with "busy" work, fitting new curtains or changing the location of the furniture.

Then she began to feel some quite acute pains. She had read popular articles on cancer, and she found that she had a number of the symptoms reported as ominous. She kept the secret to herself for a number of weeks, but the pains got worse and finally she asked one of her acquaintances to recommend a doctor to her. She went to him for an examination. He told her she did not have cancer, and that, besides, her heart, blood pressure, and digestion were those of a high-school girl!

This brought her to her senses. She awoke to the realization that fulfillment of life depends to a very great extent upon commitment to basic worthwhile projects that call forth one's energies and eager interests, and that keep one's attention from bogging down in self-diagnosis and self-pity.

On the next day after the doctor's report, she started looking for a position. She told the employment agency that she wanted one of two things—either a full-time position at a high salary, or a part-time position at some exceedingly fascinating and absorbing kind of work. High-paid full-time jobs for women over 50 were not abundant in that town, but it happened that a man who was doing research work was actively and eagerly seeking for just the kind of capacities and abilities in which this woman excelled. She took a half-time job with him, at less pay per hour than she had been getting for years past, but at a kind of work that she found fascinating and intensely absorbing. She also accepted some overtures that local organizations in her city had been making to her; she thus became active once more in civic work. Just at this time, her son and her daughter each fell deeply in love, and she devoted herself actively to bringing about satisfactory weddings. Then, quite promptly afterwards, she went to work at becoming three times a grandmother.

In her new secretarial position, she has not missed a single day on account of ill health for five years now. This means not merely that her physical condition is outstandingly good; her mental health has flourished as a result of having a life crammed full of creative, worthwhile projects.

RELIGION CAN BE THE GREAT PROJECT FOR THE LATER YEARS

What is your church doing for those in later life?

Is there a lively, vigorous, interesting class for elderly people in the Church School? If not, why not organize one? If there *is* such a group, how about taking a fresh look at its activities in order to see how it can serve the fully mature group more adequately? Are all the older members of the congregation fully enlisted in such activities? Can the pastor provide a complete list of all such people, with notations about their special interests, their physical status, and their willingness and ability to be a part of creatively cooperative activities for this age group?

In India, it has come to be recognized by many wise teachers that the life of any person can be divided into three great epochs. First, up to the time of marriage, is the period of preparation and training. The sojourner in this life is getting an education, is learning his trade or profession, is seeking out his life partner. Then comes the middle epoch of life, during which the main responsibilities are rearing a family and maintaining a home where the children can be adequately prepared for life. But when this second stage is finished, the Indians recognize that the pilgrim through life has come to a point of release, in which he can devote himself with all his heart and mind and soul to the cultivation of spiritual knowledge and wisdom.

It is at this point that the increased assurance of continued life beyond the grave has powerful effect. If personality were extinguished when the aged body is laid aside, then these later decades might come to be thought of as the time of decline and decay. Many people who have not yet realized the assurance of deathless life have drifted into the sad and worn out resignation of thus regarding the later years. But if death is the gateway to ongoing life, then the person who has reached the high maturity of the later years is in a position to prepare himself for the great journey and the great adventure of life beyond the gates of death.

Here is one point at which our churches could render far more effective and soul-building service than most of them have been doing. How about this question in your own church? Is your pastor fully alive to the opportunity for spiritual growth that these later years afford? Are the people in these golden-age brackets themselves fully profiting by the leisure that has been given them for spiritual research and spiritual growth?

THE LEISURE YEARS CAN BE THE REWARDING YEARS

All of us grow old if we live long enough. By seeing the problem in full perspective, we may realize that these riper years give opportunity for high fulfillment of the earth phase of our spiritual adventure.

Devotion to projects can bring fulfillment in the later years. Hardships do have to be met; they are an essential feature in every life-fulfilling project. Financial difficulties may stand out —and there are wise ways of dealing with them. The happiest people in later life are those who have found channels for creative activity. You may find help in that by allying yourself with the right organization. And it is important to use modern resources for staying healthy.

One mother, after her two children had left home and when she had retired from her secretarial position, began to think that she had cancer. But she discovered that her real disease was boredom. Three grandchildren, a new professional position, and civic activities, restored her life to rich happiness.

Religion can be the great project for the later years. What is your church doing to help people, in their riper decades, to prepare for the next stage in the spiritual adventure?

Chapter 16

How to Go Forward
in Life Everlasting

WE ARE ALREADY IN THE MIDST OF EVERLASTING LIFE

We are embarked on a soul-stirring adventure. It is far more rational to believe that life goes on beyond death than to believe that our consciousness will forever be extinguished when our bodies go down into the grave. Death *is* a gateway to life more magnificent.

The moment we accept this belief, we find ourselves challenged by certain tremendous consequences of survival. We come face to face with the fact that the joyfulness or painfulness of the life after death will depend upon how we have lived here in this material world.

The material world is merely a training school

This is a primary stage of our eternal education, preparatory for higher learning beyond the death of the body.

But if this is true, who are our teachers? This chapter is too brief to offer extended evidence. But five basic statements may be presented.

The first proposition is that

THE WORLD FRATERNITY IS ALREADY REAL

The reality of the world-encircling Beloved Community has been becoming more and more clear as we have progressed together from chapter to chapter in this quest of ours, especially in Chapter 8. Its members are endowed, by their membership, with the greatest attainable power *to find fulfillment of life and to bring such fulfillment* to their fellow human beings. To them are open the pathways that lead ultimately to the highest and most radiant joys conceivable, and to heights of ecstasy that lie beyond the present capacity of any of us to conceive. Their lives are allied with the creative power of the universe. The very stars in their courses minister to the fulfillment of the life of which they have become a part.

Second, the members of this greatest fraternity are endowed also with spiritual resources by means of which *they can learn to triumph over everything that is destructive.* Those who belong to this greatest fraternity are allied with the power that can win victory over every evil, every threat, and every form of suffering. Those who belong to this fellowship have the means to be delivered from all fear and from all loneliness. Poverty cannot destroy their usefulness or their happiness. Despair cannot touch them.

Third, *this fraternity traces back* into the prehistoric origins of human life on this globe, and forward forever into the future. It leads up into the very highest spiritual realms.

Fourth, this greatest fraternity cannot be reduced to terms of any earthly religion, creed, or leader. *It includes not only Christ,* but also Isaiah, Buddha, Zoroaster, Zeno, Lao-tse, and the founders and major leaders of every truly great religious faith.

Fifth, *no one can admit you or me* into this greatest fraternity unless we ourselves fulfill the basic requirements of membership. And in so far as we *do* fulfill those requirements, no one can keep you or me out.

If those five propositions are valid, then the existence of this brotherhood is the supremely important fact for every one of us who seeks fulfillment of life. How can you and I join this greatest fraternity?

The first requirement is:

WE MUST DEDICATE OUR LIVES TO FULFILLMENT OF LIFE FOR ALL

Let us suppose that any one of us should say to himself:

So far as lies within my power, I shall seek to make every action of my life such as may best serve to bring rich life and joyous growth to every human being whose life that act may influence.

Even more simply, suppose that you and I renewed our dedication every morning, in a spontaneous prayer along this line:

Help me to make every act of mine today serve to enrich the lives of those it touches.

To the extent that you or I make such a resolve and offer daily such a prayer, and then proceed to live up to the ideal thus expressed, we put ourselves into basic harmony with all the other human (and superhuman) beings who are similarly dedicated. Whenever two persons so committed become aware of one another, they (as a matter of course) begin applying this spirit of understanding and cooperation to their relations with one another. That means that they will be teaming up in their service of their fellow men. Such teams, of course, will seek to cooperate with other teams, so that a greater and greater organization naturally evolves.

Let us suppose that there is a group of people in which more and more of the members carry out these ideals more and

more wholeheartedly and consistently. What will happen in
such a group? No member will hold resentment, antagonism,
or enmity against any other member, nor even against any outsider. Each member will be wholeheartedly dedicated to promoting, both in the group and universally, the brotherhood of
mankind, the world-wide Kingdom of Heaven on earth that
was dreamed of by the Hebrew prophets, preached by Jesus,
and sought by the greatest spiritual leaders of all ages.

Heaven has been defined as "a social state in which all freely
and joyously work together for the common good." Under that
definition, we do not need to die in order to enter into heaven.
We need only to begin living the heavenly life in order to make
real in our own behavior the ideals of the Beloved Community. To the extent that you and I achieve this, a segment of
heaven has begun to grow up around us.

Wholehearted dedication to world brotherhood, by starting
in our own immediate circle of human contacts, is thus the
first inexorable requirement for membership in the Greatest
Fraternity. Let us now take a candid and honest look at the
second requirement: namely, that

EVERYONE ACCEPTED INTO THIS BROTHERHOOD MUST BE DEDICATED TO THE PURSUIT OF TRUTH

Let me bring to bear at this point an experience of my own
college days that has left a lasting impression on my life. When
I entered college I was a fundamentalist. I believed that the
Bible was inspired word by word, from cover to cover. But
during my college years my studies of psychology, economics,
and philosophy—and even my study of the Bible itself—loosened
and finally shattered my religious beliefs. I was converted to
atheism. I wrote a letter to my father telling him that I was
an emancipated spirit who no longer believed either in God
or a future life.

My father wrote me a letter in which he expressed his deep
distress that I had thus repudiated the faith in which he and

my mother had reared me. But he ended with these words: "There is one thing on which we can agree: *We will follow the truth wherever it leads us.*"

When I read that sentence my heart surged to meet my father's. I found myself crying out: "Yes, Dad; certainly! We *will* follow the truth wherever it leads us."

Shortly after my conversion to atheism, I talked with one of my professors. I remarked to him that of course no intelligent person any longer believed in God, or in the future life. The professor looked at me quizzically: "Have you ever read any psychical research?" he asked.

"Huh, that stuff!" I exclaimed, because I never *had* read any of it. But under the impetus of my father's injunction to follow the truth with unflinching honesty, wherever it leads, I went to the college library and secured a copy of F. W. H. Myers' two-volume book entitled *Human Personality and Its Survival of Bodily Death.**

I started reading it with a rather supercilious condescension. But I had not gotten far before I had to revise my opinion. It became increasingly evident that Myers was a scientist. He had collected hundreds of cases. He had analyzed them dispassionately and impartially. Before I had finished my study of his two volumes, I found that the burden of proof had shifted. I now had to take the position that I would accept the reality of life after death unless and until the contrary was proven.

The spiritual world, in which we are moving through this adventure magnificent, is infinitely vast. To learn more and more about the spiritual universe, and to discover more and more fully the growing life that we are destined to live in it, is the assignment that has been given to each one of us by virtue of the fact that we have been born.

And because we love the truth so dearly, and hunger for

---

* F. W. H. Myers, *Human Personality and Its Survival of Bodily Death,* 2 vols. (New York: Longmans Green and Co., Inc. Reprinted, 1954).

it so deeply, *we shall repudiate all fraud and all pretense.* We shall seek to free ourselves from superstition, from gullibility, and from any and every form of cheating.

All truth is one. Every dedicated seeker, in so far as he is fully committed to the quest for truth, finds himself to be allied with other seekers. The wealth of truth that they and others have gathered is their common heritage. Free from all self-seeking, they unite to promote the common goal. Nineteen hundred years ago, Jesus said:

Ye shall know the truth, and the truth shall make you free. Loyalty to liberating truth is therefore an essential requirement for membership in the greatest fraternity in the world.

This second requirement—seeking the truth fearlessly— brings us face to face with the third essential: namely

THE TRUE ASPIRANT ACCEPTS SPIRITUAL DISCIPLINE

Every effective social, psychological, scientific, business, military, and particularly spiritual undertaking requires the acceptance of specific and quite rigorous rules, without which the highest objectives of such enterprises can never be fully attained. To conduct one's life in accordance with such rules is what is meant by *discipline.*

If you are a sincere and earnest aspirant to become a full member of the Greatest Fraternity, use listening prayer to examine your own personal life and habits. In profound physical, intellectual, and emotional relaxation, ask yourself this question: "What minor (or major) vices of mine may possibly be reducing the effectiveness of my services to the supreme spiritual project?" The putting of that question should be regarded in the light of the friendly action of a comrade who helps you remove a sliver or a thorn from your hand; or, in more serious cases, of the kindly surgeon who (at your own request or with your consent) cuts out a tumor that otherwise might damage your health and even menace your life.

Over and above the first three requirements stands the fourth:

THE SEEKER FOR INITIATION MUST DEVELOP PROGRESSIVELY HIS SPIRITUAL PERCEPTIONS

How is the quest for truth related to the cultivation of spiritual awareness? Let me remind you of just one of the areas in which science has already begun to demonstrate the revolutionary contributions that it is capable of making to man's spiritual welfare. Scientific proof of extrasensory perception in parapsychological laboratories has been a crucial development toward a spiritual revolution. During the past few decades, Dr. J. B. Rhine and other parapsychologists have proved beyond any reasonable doubt the reality of telepathy, clairvoyance, psychokinesis, and prerecognition. The proven reality of these ESP powers calls for a basic reorganization of human thought. This book seeks to develop a few of the revolutionary implications of these discoveries as related to prayer, to our belief in life beyond death, and to our establishment of effective working relations with spiritual reality.

We must learn to live the guided life

Jesus said repeatedly that he was being guided by the Holy Spirit, that he spoke the words and did the deeds that were given him from on high. He instructed his disciples to seek similar guidance. Paul and the other early apostles showed evidence of such guidance in the epoch-making deeds that they performed. The Society of Friends, called Quakers, provides a modern example of people who keep seeking the guidance of the Inner Light in their daily work and in all their thinking. Countless other examples could be cited.

The guidance that has been evident in the lives of such seekers has not always been clear and consistent. Yet the major achievements of those who have built up the democratic way of life, and who have sought to live in the inspired spirit of love and truth, bear testimony as to the reality of the superhuman light and power that await our seeking. If we can bring to bear on this the resources of science, so as to understand more clearly the nature of the spiritual forces that are at work, and so that we can obtain more assuredly and fully the guidance that we need from day to day, we shall thereby enter more and more fully into the Greatest Fraternity in the world.

These dreams can be realized

Granting that we live in what is actually a spiritual universe, where death is a gateway to life more magnificent, and supposing that even a small group of people become fully sensitive to spiritual guidance, and supposing further that they seek truth unflinchingly and that in everything they do they strive to make possible fulfillment of life for all concerned, then such a group will constitute a nucleus, a living center of powerful growth, in that Great Fraternity of which we have been thinking.

Since our achievement of the life magnificent calls for heroic courage, for arduous toil, and for spiritual self-discipline, let us explore in further detail some of the definite and practical actions that are open to us if we propose to go forward in the adventure magnificent.

WE CAN DO THESE THINGS

First of all, let us recognize that the Beloved Community is to be brought into realization bit by bit and step by step.

Universal brotherly love will not take possession of the world tomorrow, nor next year, nor even next century. But it is certainly a demonstrated fact that those who are dedicated to the Beloved Community can begin to bring it into realization bit by bit in their individual personal relationships and in the groups to which they belong. You and I, by using deep prayer, can progressively transform our relationships to the people with whom we live and work. We can more and more make brotherly love and creative cooperation effective in these relationships. And as we do, we shall find that the Beloved Community spreads by contagion. This is the road to life magnificent.

Let us make full use of spiritual resources. This can be illustrated by taking a specific problem, and by indicating how it may be met spiritually.

Let us suppose that you encounter indifference, ridicule, or even opposition, injustice, greed, and cruelty. Those who have begun to progress spiritually in the Greatest Fraternity are sometimes called "Masters of Compassion." If we aspire toward that spiritual level we must train ourselves to use the triangle of brotherly prayer in relation to our brothers and sisters of the left-hand path. When we do, we shall begin to realize that those who try to gain riches, power, and advantages by harming others are doomed to defeat. Those who try to gain power by using fear, force, and fraud are generating the forces that will destroy them. People who are wronged, cheated and exploited, usually build up hatred and resentment against those who have thus abused them.

Hate breeds hate, anger breeds anger, fraud breeds distrust, violence breeds reprisal. This vicious spiral in which evil breeds evil has been the source of divorces, feuds, murders, riots, and wars. But anyone who has truly become a member of the Beloved Community seeks to make his life a transforming barrier against these destructive forces. Ships may be saved from sinking by watertight bulwarks. Fireproof partitions may save buildings from burning down. And so our human relations turn themselves into hate-tight bulwarks from which anger is turned back as love, and where evil is overcome by doing good.

WE COME NOW TO THE POINT OF DECISION

In this last chapter of our thinking together, we have been confronting a supreme challenge: joining the Greatest Fraternity in the world! It means difficulty, hardship, and toil. Of course it does. This is the paramount spiritual project that anyone can undertake, and every great project brings difficulty, hardship, and toil. But this initiation that is held out to us offers also the road to the richest and most joyous fulfillment of life that anyone can achieve.

Under the conditions that we have been setting forth in this chapter, it is evident that your membership and mine in this Greatest Fraternity will be a matter of degree. Some of us will gain only tiny flashes of awareness, which will be with us for only brief moments of time, and which will then fade back into the light of common day. These glimpses of the spiritual life that opens up before us can be expanded and developed if we are sufficiently devoted to the great undertaking. Some of you have already spent long and arduous periods of search, in which your souls have been expanded and in which you have become more and more powerfully aware of your membership in this supreme fellowship. There are no limits to the distance to which any one of us can progress if we dedicate our hearts, minds and lives to the undertaking.

But that glorious achievement is not something vague and general. Each one of us must have his or her own self-chosen and God-guided program of action. What do you propose to do, during the days immediately to come, in order that the impulse and the illumination that you have found may not evaporate into vain and unfulfilled memories?

Become a link in an infinite chain

The human and superhuman beings who seek to be sons and daughters of God may well be thought of as a chain made up of living links. Every one of us who becomes initiated stretches up one hand to his elder brothers in the spirit—his leaders and teachers of the spiritual life. We seek from these who have gone higher than we in the spiritual quest the guidance and inspiration by means of which we may find our own path upward and onward.

But if we are to become living links in the spiritual chain, we must stretch out our other hand also to our brothers and sisters of the spirit. We must be ready to give as we have received. We must be willing to pass on to other climbers the spiritual inspiration, illumination, and shared strength by means of which they too may continue to mount the steep ascent of heaven.

Each link in the spiritual chain may be thought of as though he were an electric bulb, through which current flows and becomes luminous in shining light. But suppose that an electric light bulb were conscious, and were to say: "All the current that flows in through my positive pole keeps flowing out again through my negative pole. What a waste! How much better off I would be if I could turn both of my terminals into positive poles and take in current through both."

We all know how foolish this would be. This greedy electric bulb would turn stone dark and cold. He would neither receive nor give electric current or light. Only by letting the current flow out again as it flows in can the power and the glory be experienced.

Try the following experiment during the next seven days. Every night, just before you drop off to sleep, say to yourself:

Tomorrow I shall be watching alertly for anyone who can enlighten me about the life of the spirit. I shall be humbly receptive and teachable when my teacher appears. And I shall be watching alertly also for anyone who is hungry for spiritual encouragement, sympathy, and understanding. I shall respond self-forgetfully to any outreaching by those who need the grasp of a helping hand.

Make a note of that experiment when you start it. Then make a note of the results which come to you out of it.

One further concrete and practical step is of urgent importance at this point:

Unite your life with a spiritually active group

To become an active member of some spiritually inspired organization in which the purposes of the Greatest Fraternity are being promoted is one of the most effective helps that most of us can find in this pilgrimage of ours. Seek out the church or the spiritual fellowship in which you find embodied ideals to which your spirit responds with quickened ardor and joy.

In your inner consciousness, a decision has been taking shape. What is to be your reaction to the supreme challenge? We may each of us find more clearly his own answer to that question if we seek it truly and openheartedly by means of—

LISTENING PRAYER IN SHARED COMMUNION

To the extent that you have carried out the spiritual exercises that have been set forth in the earlier chapters of this book, you have been learning more and more about how to relax profoundly, and about how, in that profoundly relaxed state, to receive illumination and to give authoritative instructions to your own unconscious mind, so as to bring your deepest attitudes into line with your own highest purposes. In confronting the supreme challenge of the spiritual life, you may find it helpful to enter into the profoundly relaxed state, and then to reach out, in shared communion, into the oneness of spirit where all our hearts and minds meet. In that shared consciousness, open your mind and ask the question: "What must *I* do in order that the purposes of the spiritual brotherhood may find greater and greater fulfillment through me and through my life?"

In preparation for that communion, put your feet flat on the floor and rest your hands limply on your lap, or take whatever other position you may find makes it easiest for you to forget your body. Close your eyes.

Now, turn your thoughts to the recollection of the deepest feelings of relaxation, of calm, and of peace that you have experienced in any previous period of autoconditioning, of listening prayer, or of deep prayer. Count silently and slowly to yourself, from one to five, with pauses between the numbers. As you count, turn your attention to feeling inwardly the depth of the peace that passes all understanding.

In the profound state of deep relaxation that you will thus reach, pause for several minutes and listen to the voice of silence. Open your heart and your mind to receive the guidance that you seek about how you can best and most fully go forward in the life everlasting.

ACTION HERE AND NOW

In the light of the facts and the thinking that have been reviewed thus far in this book, a simple and promising program of action emerges. The following steps can well be taken, in the light of the epoch-making discoveries that have been coming out in psychical research:

1. Let us study with keen interest the reports that have already been published by psychic researchers in this field, so as to become fully aware of the evidence that throws light upon personal survival beyond the grave.

2. Let us follow with active sympathy, but also with alert critical understanding, the reports that psychic explorers make about their difficult and often dangerous experiments in seeking to expand still further their knowledge—and ours—of the psychic and spiritual worlds.

3. Let us seek to discover and apply effective measures by means of which people like ourselves can live our lives in the light of eternity. Let us learn to live with full awareness of the fact that life goes on beyond the grave. Let us live with full awareness that we are surrounded by a great host of witnesses, and that our lives can be inspired and guided by understanding and making full use of our normal faculties and of the creative contacts that are possible to every dedicated and spiritually sensitive person. Let us cultivate, to the highest degree attainable, both listening prayer and deep prayer.

4. Let us begin, right now, to cultivate the kind of character that will make us fit to go forward and to serve others in the spiritual life, both here and beyond the grave. Let us learn to enter creatively into the lives of our fellow men, so that we may participate in rich and joyous friendships, be partners in productive undertakings, and be worthy of being loved in our families and our communities; and that we may be citizens who help to build democracy in our local governments, our nations, and our world.

TO US HAS BEEN OPENED UP A SHINING VISION

We began this book with our problems. We started with the fact that many of us had at times felt lonely, discouraged, and defeated. Many of us had often felt hungry in spirit for something solid to believe in. We had been confronted by the great enigmas of life and death. We had undergone bereavement. At times we had felt depressed, disheartened, and guilty. We had been perplexed about the meaning of life, and about how we might learn to live radiantly.

The answers have now taken shape, out of the pages through which we have passed together. We have learned that the Power above all human power and the Wisdom above all human wisdom are accessible to us, and that we can learn to bring them into our lives at every time of need. We have learned that, aided by that Power, and guided by that Wisdom, we need never again feel defeated. We have learned that death is merely a gateway to life more magnificent. We have become aware of a supreme fellowship enfolding us. It is the Great Fraternity to which you and I are invited to accept conscious initiation. We have only to fulfill the basic conditions of brotherly love, of unwavering truth-seeking, and of spiritual awakening.

The great adventure to which we are summoned is neither painless nor easy. Yet, realizing the hardships, difficulties and dangers, with Divine courage we press forward on our quest for light and truth. Uniting our hearts, we dedicate all that we are and have to living the Life Magnificent here and now.